JERKY

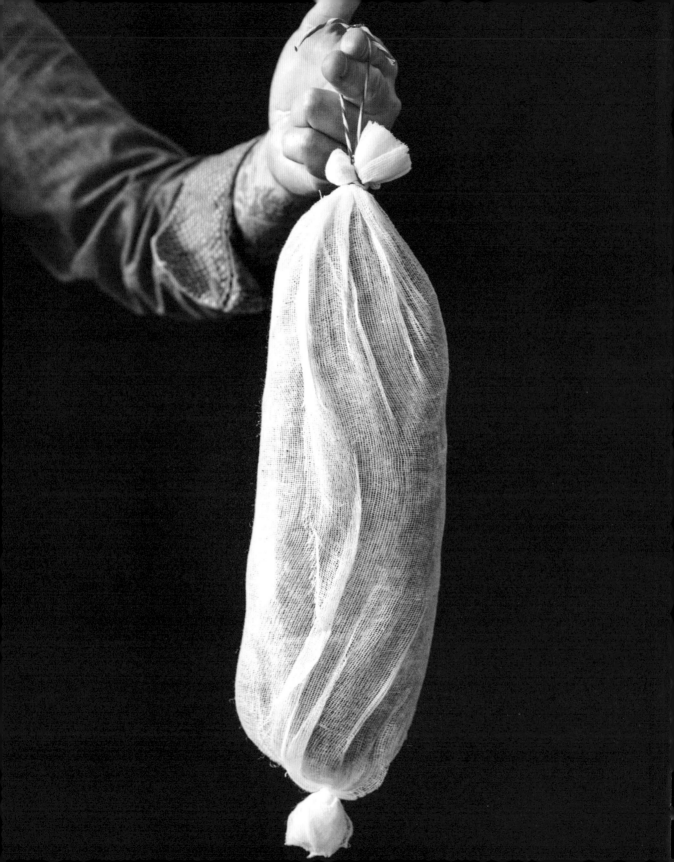

JERKY

THE FATTED CALF'S

GUIDE TO PRESERVING & COOKING
DRIED MEATY GOODS

**TAYLOR BOETTICHER
& TOPONIA MILLER**

PHOTOGRAPHS BY
ED ANDERSON

TEN SPEED PRESS
California | New York

CONTENTS

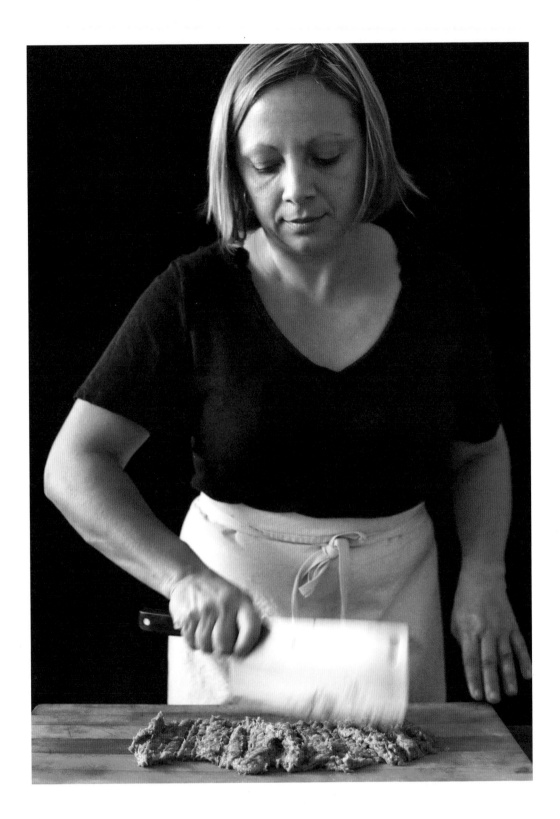

MAGIC MEAT

by Toponia Miller

Somewhere around thirty thousand feet my stomach growled. It had been a mad dash in slow traffic from our home in Sonoma to the chaotic Southwest terminal in Oakland with few edible enticements between ticketing and the gate. For the duration of my two-hour trip, surely I could resist the in-flight temptations of turkey wraps and tepid sushi.

But once aloft, the low-blood-sugar headache began to set in. As someone who thinks about food virtually nonstop and feeds others for a living, how can I forget to feed myself? Picky person that I am, I usually provision myself well for even a short jaunt and cursed my insistence on "traveling light" this time. My stomach growled aloud. Why had I brought only cooking magazines to peruse? Surely, I must have something I could eat. I shimmied my pack out from under the seat in front of me and rummaged through its contents: toiletries, miscellaneous chargers and cords, a notepad, and then, crammed into a zippered pocket, a half-eaten packet of beef jerky. Salvation!

How long had it quietly ridden with me through my daily routine, unnoticed? A month, maybe more, forgotten in a subcompartment after a trek through the coastal woodlands. Despite the passage of time and neglect, its scent was irresistible. I ripped off piece after piece and shoved them in my mouth. The salty, slightly smoky strips brought instant relief. Their texture, leathery yet yielding, was a marvel. My seatmates side-eyed me as I chewed loudly. No matter to me, they could stare all they liked. I was going to ride the protein high of this magic meat all the way to Albuquerque.

FALLING FOR JERKY

Love is a curious thing. I wasn't always so hung up on jerky. In fact, I had quite a collection of jerky prejudices and looked down my upturned nose at the stuff. The convenience store bins of hermetically sealed sticks of mystery meat held no allure.

I had my first jerky encounter when I was twenty-two. I was cooking at a café during the daylight hours but often picked up catering work at night. After one of these marathon work binges I crawled into bed, too tired to be bothered with supper. When I awoke the next morning, there was a very pressing need for both caffeine and sustenance. While the pot of coffee was brewing, I rummaged in the fridge, finding only soggy lettuces, blackened avocado halves, and other forgotten relics from the farmers' market. A three-day-old baguette could be weaponized more effortlessly than eaten.

Then I spied the bag that Taylor had left on the kitchen table for me. He had just started working at a local meat market. "You have to try the beef jerky we're making," he had told me days earlier. Considering my limited options and suppressing the priggish part of me that felt this was a nutritionally dicey breakfast, I poured myself a giant steaming mug of coffee topped with cream and dove into the greasy bag. To my surprise, I discovered that caffeine + beefy, salty, sweet protein = amazing. I ate it all and I wanted more.

I came to rely on that jerky as a quick pick-me-up when a meal was not in the cards. It was portable and could be conveniently consumed while running errands or dashing between jobs. I found it more satisfying than other snack foods. And unlike the pieces of fruit that were forever rotting in the innards of my purse, the jerky stayed well preserved for weeks.

We tend to think of jerky as a fairly ubiquitous American food, but the love of jerky knows no borders. When Taylor and I scraped together enough money to travel abroad, we realized that there was a whole world of jerky out there. In tiny butcher shops in Italy we found baskets of highly spiced pork jerky. On an island off the coast of Vietnam we saw strips of beef drying in the sun. Even in our own backyard we could sample Ethiopian *quanta* and Thai *moo dat diow*.

JERKY GENESIS

One morning, as I watched my dogs excitedly nosing a flattened, sun-parched fence lizard, I thought about how our ancestors, wandering the cradle of civilization, must have similarly stumbled upon dried-up critters and, like the toddlers of the human race, discerned them to be a reasonable foodstuff only after putting them in their mouths. Perhaps not delicious by today's standards, they were at least edible. In this way, perhaps, the first primitive jerky was born.

The word *jerky* is a bastardized version of *ch'arki*, meaning simply "salted meat" in Quechua, the language spoken by the Incas, the indigenous peoples of the South American Andean highlands. But the Incas weren't alone in their love of jerky. Many traditional cultures perfected drying salted meat in the hot sun or over a slow-burning fire as a means to preserve their kill. Learning to preserve protein for later consumption had a profound impact on human evolution.

It seems wherever humans went, jerky went with them. Long before we settled down into pastoral life, these rustic, thin strips of dried meat provided a portable, shelf-stable protein option for early nomadic cultures. Later, spices were added both for flavor and as an additional preservative. As people marched across the globe, their jerky picked up a little aromatic herb here and a spicy chile there. People learned to cook with jerky and other dried meats. Jerky became a handy kitchen staple that could be added to everything from salads to stir-fries and stews.

Sometime after the Industrial Age, things went awry for simple, nutritious jerky. Meat processing migrated from small farms and local abattoirs to large centralized facilities. These industrial meat-processing plants used by-products to produce a variety of snack meats loaded with chemical preservatives and sugars. These jerky-type products were pumped into the marketplace, often replacing traditionally dried meats. Dark days for jerky indeed.

A JERKY OF OUR OWN

In 2003, Taylor and I threw our hats in the ring and started up our little meat biz, The Fatted Calf. We knew jerky was a menu must. When we were developing our signature jerky, we wanted to create something distinct yet still simple and irresistible, and definitely more sophisticated than your average convenience-store offering. We wanted to be able to taste the meat—the high-quality, locally raised beef—and not a bunch of weird additives or trendy ingredients.

We began every week by slicing sheets of rosy-red beef. Good-quality sea salt and freshly ground black pepper were the only spices it needed. Molasses provided it with a rich, bitter sweetness, while bourbon added an elegant aroma and subtly tangy flavor. A little smoke from slowly burning fruitwood perfumed it and gave it a taste reminiscent of a good steak. It was the jerky of our dreams, and it became one of the most popular items at our two shops. Fresh from the dehydrator, slightly warm, and chewy-tender, it still makes me swoon.

WHOLE LOTTA JERKY LOVE

Love takes you to places you never thought you'd go. While our own jerky holds a special place in our hearts, we are total meat tramps. We'll never forget our first mouthful of the Mexican specialty *machaca*. Who could resist the charms of a lemongrass-scented slice of Vietnamese *thit bo kho*? We'd happily cross an ocean for Spain's *tasajo*. There is a lot of jerky to love.

Love beckons you to try something new. We can't spend all of our time chasing jerky around the globe, so often we are at home in our kitchen trying our hand at Korean *yukpo*, drying duck breasts in our garage, or experimenting with amaro as a seasoning for pork jerky. We've built a life with jerky. There is meat in our refrigerator now awaiting its jerky transformation. A cookie jar of jerky sits on our counter, ready for a trip to the beach or to enjoy with a cocktail as a prelude to dinner. We rarely leave the house without a pouchful, and when we do travel, we often bring the gift of jerky with us.

When you truly love something, you can't seem to shut up about it. You want to shout it from the rooftop. You want to spell its name in lights. Or better yet, write a book about it. This is our jerky love story.

JERKY BASICS

Making your own jerky and dried meats is an extremely rewarding process. With a minimal capital expenditure and a little bit of time, you can generate a wealth of meaty treats suited to your taste.

Making the best jerky is simple. Use good-quality meat and all-natural seasonings and the result will be the best, freshest, and most wholesome jerky. Forget the mystery meat you find in stores. One of the best things about making your own jerky and other dried meats is that you can choose your raw ingredients and how to prepare them. You can make the choices that resonate with your personal food philosophy. You can source your meat from your favorite farmer or trusted butcher; seek out meat that is pastured, humanely raised, or grass-fed; or use wild game and season it with natural spices and fresh herbs to create a delicious, protein-rich, anytime treat that you feel good about eating. If you are going to make the effort to DIY, you might as well go with the good stuff.

SELECTING MEAT FOR JERKY

Jerky can be made from almost any cut of any animal, but there are a few general principles we adhere to when selecting meat for jerky.

- Always use good-quality, fresh meat to prepare jerky. No matter what type of animal or which cut you use, quality and freshness make a big difference in the flavor of the finished jerky. The drying process intensifies the flavors in the meat. Anything questionable will only become more suspect when dehydrated. Look for cuts that are firm and vibrantly colored, with bright white fat.

- Meat from the leaner hind quarter or leg area of most animals is typically preferred for making jerky. These tougher and often less expensive cuts are chosen both because they are flavorful and because they have very little intramuscular fat, which allows them to dry more quickly and evenly. However, simply because leaner cuts tend to be preferable, don't fear a little fat on your jerky meat. Although most of the recipes in this book call for well-trimmed meats, a small amount of fat can actually enhance the flavor and add a suppleness to the texture of your jerky. Fat does have a higher water content than lean meat, which means it will take longer to dry or will not dry as well as leaner meat; this can somewhat reduce the shelf life of your jerky. But if you are a jerky lover, you'll eat it fast enough that this won't be an issue!

- Select large pieces of meat. Since you will be cutting long strips or slices, start with a piece of meat that is suitably large and thick.

- Start with a cut that weighs slightly more than the recipe calls for, to give yourself a little wiggle room. You will lose some meat in the trimming process.

TRIMMING AND CUTTING

Most of the recipes in this book call for meat to be prepared in "strips"—stick-like lengths of a fairly uniform diameter—or "slices"—wide, flat pieces. There are a number of ways to trim and slice meat into strips or slices for drying, but here are a few simple tips to keep in mind.

- Use a sharp knife. A dull blade will slow you down and make cutting meat a chore.

- Trim the meat of most external fat before slicing or cutting it into strips. For most types of jerky, you want no more than ¼ inch (6 mm) of external fat.

- To help achieve thinner slices, freeze the meat for 1 to 1½ hours so it is very firm but not frozen solid.

- If you are slicing the meat, you generally want to cut against the grain into slices ⅛ to ¼ inch (3 to 6 mm) thick.

- If you have access to an electric meat slicer, it will make quick work of slicing meat for jerky. Alternatively, consider asking your butcher to slice the meat for you.

- If the meat slices seem a little too thick or are of an uneven thickness, lightly pound them or butterfly the thickest portion to achieve a more uniform thickness.

- If you are cutting meat strips or sticks, you generally want to cut them so they are ½ inch (12 mm) in diameter.

- Don't waste the trim! Meat trim is excellent when ground for burgers or chopped for use in chili or soups. Fat trim can be chopped and rendered to use for cooking.

SLICES

STRIPS

WITH IT OR AGAINST IT?

In meat speak, "the grain" refers to the direction in which the muscle fibers align. If you cut parallel to the long muscle fibers, you are cutting "with the grain." If you are cut across or perpendicular to the muscle fibers, you are slicing "against the grain." Generally speaking, cutting meat against the grain makes it meat easier to chew because you are slicing through the muscle fibers, thereby shortening them and making less work for your teeth. For some cuts of meat, cutting with or against the grain doesn't make a significant difference. For example, a boneless pork loin is extremely tender and will remain so no matter how it is sliced. But more exercised muscles, such as leg cuts, have longer fibers, and you will want to cut across them. To determine the direction of the grain, look closely at the cut of meat and you will usually see a subtle striation. To cut against the grain, hold your knife perpendicular to the lines and slice across.

BEEF AND BISON

Beef and bison have a similar muscular structure and are interchangeable for the purposes of jerky making. However, bison, also referred to as buffalo, is naturally leaner and higher in protein than most beef. It also has a somewhat nuttier and sweeter flavor than beef, which we find to be more unctuous and savory. Both make excellent jerky.

THE ROUND

Located in the hindquarter of beef and bison, the round is comprised of the top round, bottom round, and eye of round. This well-used muscle group makes for tough and lean yet flavorful cuts that are perfect for drying.

The eye of round is the cylindrical muscle that resembles a plump tenderloin. A whole eye of round weighs between 3 and 5 pounds (1.4 and 2.3 kg), requires minimal trimming, and has very little intramuscular fat. It is best sliced thinly against the grain or dried whole as in the recipe for Brési (page 90).

Top round is a little more marbled and will require a bit of trimming. It is also larger than the eye of round and the top round, usually weighing 8 to 10 pounds (3.6 to 4.5 kg). Split it in half lengthwise before cutting slices or strips for jerky.

The bottom round has a little more intermuscular and intramuscular fat than the eye of round but less than top round. A whole bottom round usually weighs 6 to 8 pounds (2.7 to 3.6 kg) and will require some trimming. To make slicing easier, cut the whole muscle in half crosswise before cutting strips or slices.

BRISKET

The brisket comes from the breast area of beef and bison, between the forelegs. A whole brisket is fairly large, weighing 10 to 12 pounds (4.5 to 5.4 kg), and consists of the well-marbled "point" end and the "flat" end. Briskets vary greatly in their intramuscular fat, or marbling, as well as in their intermuscular fat, or the amount of fat on the outside of the muscle. For the purposes of making jerky, you will want to stick with the brisket flat, which is more uniform in shape and leaner than the point. It can be purchased separately or easily cut away from the whole. You may need to trim the brisket further so that the exterior fat cap is less than ¼ inch (6 mm) thick.

Brisket breaks from the conventional notion that meats for drying need to be hyperlean. Although its fat content can increase the time it takes to dry and slightly decrease its shelf life, it makes for a texturally interesting and quite delicious jerky. We like to use brisket in recipes such as Pocket Pastrami (page 61), because its fat is a good foil for the bold pastrami spicing, and in Carne Seca (page 31) because its texture makes it easy to shred into strands for Machaca (page 82).

GROUND

Ground beef and bison can also be used for some types of jerky. You will want to use ground beef or bison that is at least 85 percent lean and finely ground twice. To ensure the correct grind, we recommend working with your butcher or buying whole cuts and grinding them yourself. That said, most commercially available ground beef has been twice-ground. Before seasoning, chop the ground meat further using a cleaver or chef's knife to achieve a uniform consistency.

PORK AND WILD BOAR

Pork and wild boar share a similar muscle structure, but their flavor and fat can be vastly different. Farm-raised pork is less chewy than many other meats, and its mild flavor is a versatile canvas for a variety of seasonings. It's a popular jerky option, especially for *coppiette* in Italy and for a variety of different dried meats throughout Asia. Its softer texture can make it a little tricky to slice, so chilling or partially freezing the meat before slicing is recommended. It is also usually a bit fattier than most meats, so it will require a little more trimming.

Wild boar, the ancestor of most domestic pork, has a more assertive and nutty flavor than its farmyard cousin. This shy, surly beast boasts meat that is darker in color, leaner, and sometimes tougher than pork because its muscles receive plenty of exercise roaming in the wild and foraging for its supper. It also tends to be firmer than pork, so it is a little easier to slice and takes less time to dry.

LEG OR FRESH HAM

The hind leg of the pig and boar is referred to as the "ham" or "fresh ham," not to be confused with cured, smoked, or cooked ham that is ready to eat. The ham can be divided into the shank end or lower end and the sirloin or top part. The shank end tends to be sinewy, so if used for jerky, it requires a bit of trimming. The sirloin, which weighs roughly 3 to 4 pounds (1.4 to 1.8 kg), is composed of several smaller muscles, all of which are fairly lean with minimal sinew and intramuscular fat, making them excellent candidates for cutting into slices or strips for drying.

LOIN

Boneless loin of pork, though more expensive than pork leg cuts, makes for very lean, elegant, and easy-to-slice meat for drying. A whole boneless center-cut loin weighs between 4 and 6 pounds (1.8 and 2.7 kg) and is 12 to 15 inches (30 to 38 cm) long. Its length makes it perfect for cutting long strips for *coppiette*. It can also be sliced crosswise into rounds. Boar loin is similarly lean and tender but can vary in size more greatly than pork.

GROUND

Ground pork and boar, when rolled out into thin sheets, make excellent jerky. You will need pork that is at least 85 percent lean, ideally from the leg. It should be ground finely and then chopped using a cleaver or chef's knife to achieve a uniform consistency.

DEER, ANTELOPE, GOAT, AND LAMB

Smaller ruminants, such as goat, lamb, deer, and even antelope, are used throughout the world to make a diverse assortment of dried-meat delicacies. Although they vary in size and flavor, they share many similar characteristics, including basic muscular structure. They are naturally lean and usually require minimum trimming. Their meat tends to be robustly flavored and is a good match for bold seasonings and spices.

LEG

Boneless leg cuts are very lean with little intramuscular fat, making them good choices for drying. Just trim away any sinew from the shank end before cutting into strips or slices.

LOIN

Lean loin requires almost no trimming and can be cut lengthwise into strips or sliced crosswise into rounds.

BASIC JERKY FORMULA

At its most basic, jerky is just meat that is salted and dried. You can use this basic jerky formula to create recipes using whatever flavorings you like. Just keep in mind that if you are using soy sauce, fish sauce, or other seasonings that contain or mimic saltiness, you will need to adjust the amount of salt.

2 pounds (910 g) trimmed meat, sliced ⅛ to ¼ inch (3 to 6 mm) thick against the grain or cut into strips ½ inch (12 mm) in diameter

+ 1 tablespoon plus 1 teaspoon salt

= about 1 pound (450 g) jerky

SALT

In addition to enhancing the meat's savoriness, salt is crucial for preservation. Salt creates a hostile environment for harmful microorganisms because it dehydrates bacterial cells and thereby inhibits the growth of bacteria that can cause spoilage.

We recommend fine sea salt for making jerky because it easily disperses over the surface of the meat, is readily absorbed, and has a pleasant, natural flavor. If you prefer to use kosher salt or another type of coarse salt, you may need to use slightly more salt than called for in the recipes in this book.

When air-drying some larger, whole cuts of meat, we recommend also using curing salt #2, which contains a small percentage of sodium nitrate. Sodium nitrate is an extremely effective antimicrobial agent and antioxidant that prevents the growth of the most harmful bacteria, including those that can cause botulism.

SPICES

Spices captivate our senses with their alluring fragrance, trigger our taste memories, and are the heart and soul of many traditional regional styles of jerky. We generally recommend starting with whole spices (which stay fresh far longer than preground), then toasting and grinding them as needed for each recipe. Lightly toasting spices releases their essential oils and intensifies their flavors. We either toast spices in a dry skillet over low heat or on a baking sheet in 325°F (165°C) oven for 3 to 5 minutes, until they give off an aroma. Allow the spices to cool, then grind them in a spice grinder or with a mortar and pestle.

JERKY FLAVOR

When seasoning meat to make jerky, we like to think in terms of savory, spicy, sweet, herbaceous, and tangy flavors. Some of our favorite jerky recipes find a way to combine and balance all of these elements.

SPICY, HOT, AND PEPPERY
fresh and dried chiles, chile powders, peppercorns, mustard, ginger

HERBACEOUS
fresh and dried herbs (rosemary, cilantro, lemongrass), alliums (shallots, garlic, green onions)

SWEET
sugar, brown sugar, honey, molasses, apple or pear juice

SAVORY
soy sauce, fish sauce, fresh or dried mushrooms, miso, shallots, garlic, green onions, herbs, Worcestershire sauce

TANGY OR SOUR
wine, vinegar, mirin, tamarind, citrus zest and juice, bourbon, lime leaf, sake

SPECIAL EQUIPMENT

There is a glut of gadgets and gizmos available for making jerky. If you are a gearhead, there is no end to the number of contraptions you can put on your wish list, from jerky cannons to special jerky slicers. If you are a minimalist, you probably already have everything you need. But there are a few things we recommend to make jerky making simpler and more enjoyable.

- A digital electronic food scale will take the guesswork out of weighing meat for jerky preparation.
- Rimmed baking sheets fitted with wire racks are handy for oven-drying and for use with many smokers. To maximize your oven space, there are also tiered racks or jerky hangers fitted with skewers.
- A dehydrator makes the drying process a snap.
- A grill or smoker is great for hot and cold smoking when a little wood-smoke flavor is desired.
- A hanging drying net or basket is a multitiered mesh basket that can be used outdoors for sun-drying jerky or indoors for air-drying. It provides plenty of airflow while protecting the drying meat from most pests.

DRYING METHODS

When it comes to drying meat, there are many roads that more or less lead to the same destination. The goal is to preserve the meat by removing about 85 percent of its water content. When the meat is depleted of moisture, the harmful bacteria that can cause spoilage cannot grow. A dehydrator is the simplest and most reliable way to make most types of jerky, and, unless otherwise noted, it is the method we used to test the recipes in this book. If you don't have a dehydrator, however, you could use sun-drying or oven-drying methods (see pages 18 and 21). Or, if you prefer jerky with a smokier flavor, try drying your jerky over embers (see page 21). A little experimentation is part of the fun of making jerky, and often yields delicious results.

SUN-DRYING

Go back, way back, in time and connect with your primordial self by employing solar energy to dry your meat. Sun-drying was likely the first method employed to preserve meat, and it is still an effective preservation method used in many parts of the world. You may wonder, is it safe to leave raw meat sitting in the sun? Most likely, the USDA would not approve of this method. However, we have dried jerky this way and lived to tell the tale.

When sun-drying, choose a day or a succession of days when it is hot, dry, and preferably breezy and a location that receives direct, overhead sunlight for at least a few hours per day. We have had the best results with this method when the thermometer crept above 90°F (32°C), the sky was bright blue, and there were gentle winds blowing.

You will need to protect your meat from pests. The best way to do this is to use a hanging mesh dehydrating basket made expressly for the purpose of sun-drying plants, fruits, and meat. They are cheap and readily available on the Internet, so there is little reason to mess with less effective substitutes if you are interested in sun-drying. These baskets allow air to flow freely through ventilation holes while keeping the contents out of the reach of hungry critters.

Space the meat in the basket so that no meat is overlapping. Check the meat for dryness every 8 hours or so. The finished jerky will be uniform in color, leathery, and firm but still somewhat pliable. Drying times vary greatly with the weather conditions, but generally jerky will dry in 24 to 48 hours.

AIR-DRYING

A little patience can produce very fine results with air-drying. Unlike sun-drying, air-drying is done at a much lower temperature and can be done indoors. This method is best suited for drying thicker or larger cuts of meat, such as in the recipes for Tasajo con Pimentón (page 87) and Spiced Duck Breasts (page 88), rather than thin slices or strips. To air-dry, hang the meat in a dry, well-ventilated location with a relatively stable temperature, ideally between 50°F and 60°F (10°C and 16°C). Depending on the size and thickness of the cut as well as the drying conditions, air-drying can take anywhere from a few days to a year or more.

DRYING OVER EMBERS

Ah, the romance of making jerky the old-fashioned way over the glowing embers of a dying fire! Although less precise than dehydrating and requiring a little more attention than smoking (see page 24), this primitive method has a certain flair and flavor all its own. Jerky slowly dried over embers has a subtle smokiness. You can use this method to impart just a hint of smoke, as you would with cold smoking, or you can dry the jerky start to finish with the fire's residual heat.

This is best done outdoors in a fire pit or indoors in a fireplace. We like to start with a delicately aromatic wood, such as almond, alder, cherry or apple. Light a fire and let it burn down to glowing coals. Lay the meat on a rack or drape it over poles. Position the meat near enough to the coals to benefit from the heat and smoke but not so close that it cooks. Timing will vary, so be prepared to experiment and monitor the jerky's progress. It may also be necessary to stoke the fire from time to time—but what better way to spend an afternoon?

OVEN-DRYING

A home oven set to the lowest possible temperature is a perfectly simple and easy way to dry jerky. If your oven runs hot or the thermometer registers higher than 160°F (71°C), leave the oven door slightly ajar during the drying process to achieve a temperature between 140°F and 160°F (60°C and 71°C). Lay the slices of meat on a wire rack set in a rimmed baking sheet or arrange them on a jerky hanger, making sure the meat is not overlapping or touching. Place the pan in the warm oven. Rotate the pan midway through the drying process (the exact timing will depend on the type and thickness of the jerky) to ensure even drying.

USING A DEHYDRATOR

One can forgive the lack of nostalgia with this most reliable and convenient method of drying. Dehydrators are fairly simple machines, usually just a heavy plastic or metal box fitted with racks and equipped with a low-temperature heating element, an adjustable thermostat, and a fan to circulate the warm air. There is a range of good dehydrators on the market. Ideally you want something that is large enough to fit at least a couple pounds of meat but not so bulky that it won't fit on your countertop.

To use a dehydrator, simply set the temperature to 145°F (63°C). Lay the slices or strips of meat on the dehydrator racks, making sure that no pieces are overlapping. Place the racks into the dehydrator, leaving as much space as possible between them. Rotate the racks midway through the drying process to ensure even drying.

SMOKING

Smoking is another method for drying, preserving, and flavoring jerky. Wood smoke imparts a deep, rich flavor to the meat while also depositing hundreds of compounds on the surface of the meat that naturally slow the growth of harmful, spoilage-causing organisms.

Cold Smoking

Cold smoking is the addition of smoke without the addition of heat. It is mostly intended to impart a delicate smoky flavor to the meat, not cook it, and must be used in conjunction with another drying method, such as air-drying or dehydrator-drying, to fully dry the meat. For cold smoking, the meat is placed over a very low or indirect smoldering fire or in an unheated chamber into which smoke is funneled from an adjacent firebox. There are several ways to cold smoke, depending on the type of smoker. If you are using a grill or a more traditional wood-burning smoker, let your fire burn down to coals and then add soaked wood chips or a small soaked log that will smolder at a very low temperature. Electric smokers are usually equipped with a pellet- or chip-burning firebox and a heating element that can be temperature regulated.

No matter how you cold smoke, you want to try to keep the temperature of the smoker between 60°F and 80°F (16°C and 27°C). How long you cold smoke your jerky depends on how smoky you like it. Even just 20 minutes of cold smoking can infuse the meat with plenty of smoky flavor.

Hot Smoking

Hot smoking jerky fully dries the jerky at a normal drying temperature (somewhere between 140°F and 160°F [60°C and 71°C]) but with the addition of fragrant smoke. You can hot smoke jerky using any type of wood-fired or electric smoker and on most traditional wood or charcoal burning grills. We generally prefer to avoid the use of natural gas or propane smokers and grills, as gas and propane contain chemical compounds that can produce unwanted and unpleasant flavors in the finished jerky.

To hot smoke jerky, begin by lighting a wood or charcoal fire in your smoker or grill. Let the fire burn down to glowing coals. Bank the coals to produce a deep coal bed. (If you are using an electric smoker you will skip this step and just turn the smoker on.) If you are using a smaller type grill you will want to push the coals to one side of your grill so that you can smoke the jerky over indirect heat. To the coals, add chips or chunks of wood that have been thoroughly soaked in water—they should smolder rather than catch fire. When your smoker or grill reaches the correct temperature (between 140°F and 160°F [60°C and 71°C]), place the meat on the smoking racks or on a jerky hanger (see photo, page 51) in a manner that allows the smoke to circulate. Monitor the temperature and adjust the coals as needed.

GAUGING DONENESS

Waiting for your jerky to be ready to eat is the hardest part of jerky making. The water and fat content of the meat, the thickness of the strips or slices, the method and equipment you choose for drying, along with a variety of environmental factors, all impact drying times. The drying process will reduce the overall weight of the jerky by 50 to 75 percent. Finished jerky can vary from lightly dried to almost brittle, and the level of dryness you achieve is a matter of personal taste and the amount of time you plan to keep your jerky. We usually look for our finished jerky to be pliable and chewy but still tender enough to tear easily with your teeth. As you are trying new recipes and methods, it's a good idea to try small tastes of partially dried jerky so you can get a feel for doneness.

STORING JERKY

While most jerky and dried meat is relatively shelf stable at room temperature, fluctuations in humidity, exposure to light, and temperature variation can negatively affect the quality. Dried meats need to be stored in a clean, dry container, ideally with a little bit of airflow. A cookie jar, tin, or storage container with a lid that fits securely but isn't airtight is ideal. Make sure there is a little breathing room between the pieces of jerky. If the jerky is too tightly packed or overlapping, mold can occur. Be wary of zipper-lock bags, even for transport. They seal too tightly to allow airflow and can encourage mold—as we learned the hard way on a trip to the humid Florida coast. If you plan on keeping your jerky for longer than a week or two, we also encourage the use of food-safe desiccant packets. One or two packets inside the storage container with the jerky will help control the humidity level and discourage the growth of mold.

CHAPTER ONE

SIMPLE AND CLASSIC JERKY

This is an old-school, lo-fi jerky called *charqui* or *carne de sol*, depending on your locale. The depth of flavors yielded by simply baking salted beef in the hot sun are reminiscent of a superb dry-aged steak. This jerky staple is great to eat on its own or can be used as an ingredient for cooking, as in Feijoada (page 99), the popular Brazilian meat and bean stew.

For the uninitiated, sun-drying requires a leap of faith. Just bear in mind that you will need to be a little flexible with the timing since how long the meat takes to dry is weather-dependent. We highly recommend the use of a mesh drying basket (see page 18), which allows for maximum airflow during the sun-drying process while keeping the meat safely out of the reach of pests.

MEAT + SALT + SUN

MAKES ABOUT 1 POUND (450 G)

2 pounds (910 g) well-trimmed beef brisket or bottom round, sliced against the grain as thinly as possible

1½ tablespoons fine sea salt

Warm, sunny, dry weather

Massage the salt into the beef slices. Lay the slices directly onto the screens or mesh shelves of a drying basket, making sure that no slices are overlapping. Hang the basket outdoors in a well-ventilated, warm, sunny location for 24 hours.

After 24 hours, check the dryness of the jerky (see page 25). If the slices are dried to your liking, remove them from the basket. If you prefer drier jerky, continue drying, checking every 4 to 8 hours, for up to 24 more hours.

Transfer the jerky to a covered container that allows a bit of airflow and store in a cool, dark place for up to 6 weeks.

Carne seca, Spanish for "dried meat," is a specialty of the border-lands of northern Mexico and the southwestern United States. Simply seasoned with lime and mild dried Anaheim chile, this jerky is a great everyday snack as well as an essential component for Machaca (page 82) a Sonoran specialty. You can make *carne seca* in a dehydrator or oven, but we prefer the intoxicating perfume of wood smoke obtained by drying the beef with hot smoke or over the embers of a low fire.

CARNE SECA

MAKES ABOUT 1 POUND (450 G)

1 dried Anaheim or New Mexico chile

1½ tablespoons fine sea salt

2 pounds (910 g) well-trimmed beef brisket, sliced ⅛ to ¼ inch (3 to 6 mm) thick against the grain

1 lime, halved

Toast the chile in a dry skillet over medium heat for about 30 seconds per side. Allow to cool to room temperature. Stem and seed the chile, then break the pod into pieces. Using a spice grinder, pulverize the chile to a fine powder. In a small bowl, combine the chile powder and salt.

Place the sliced beef in a shallow bowl or container and season with the chile-salt mixture. Squeeze the lime over the meat. Using your hands, mix well to evenly coat the slices. Cover and refrigerate for at least 3 hours or up to overnight.

When you are ready to dry the beef, remove the meat from the refrigerator. Place the slices on the racks of your dehydrator, making sure that no slices are overlapping. Set the temperature to 145°F (63°C). Insert the racks into your dehydrator, leaving as much space as possible between them. Dehydrate for about 2½ hours, until the slices are firm but still pliable, rotating the racks front to back halfway through to ensure even drying.

Alternatively, you can use a smoker. Arrange the slices on the racks, making sure that no slices are overlapping. You want to keep the temperature in the smoker between 140°F and 160°F (60°C and 65°C). Insert the racks into the smoker, leaving as much space as possible between them. Dry the meat for about 2½ hours, until the slices are firm but still pliable, rotating the racks front to back halfway through to ensure even drying.

Allow the jerky to cool at room temperature. Transfer to a covered container that allows a bit of airflow and store in a cool, dark place for up to 6 weeks.

Beef and Worcestershire sauce are a classic pairing, and this simple yet tantalizing jerky illustrates why. Much like soy sauce or fish sauce, Worcestershire accentuates beef's depth of flavor, but it also provides a pungent, peppery, vinegary kick that keeps your mouth watering for another piece. We highly encourage you to make your own Worcestershire sauce, as it makes all the difference in this recipe.

PEPPERED BEEF WITH WORCESTERSHIRE

MAKES ABOUT 1 POUND (450 G)

2 pounds (910 g) trimmed beef bottom round, sliced ⅛ to ¼ inch (3 to 6 mm) thick against the grain

1 tablespoon fine sea salt

¼ cup (60 ml) Worcestershire Sauce (page 34)

2 teaspoons black peppercorns, coarsely ground

Place the sliced beef in a shallow bowl or container and sprinkle with the salt. Toss the slices, then add the Worcestershire sauce. Using your hands, mix well to evenly coat the slices. Cover and refrigerate for at least 3 hours or up to overnight.

When you are ready to dry the beef, remove the meat from the refrigerator. Place the slices on the racks of your dehydrator, making sure that no slices are overlapping. Sprinkle a little of the pepper onto each slice. Set the temperature to 145°F (63°C). Insert the racks into the dehydrator, leaving as much space as possible between them. Dehydrate for about 2½ hours, until the slices are firm but still pliable, rotating the racks front to back halfway through to ensure even drying.

Allow the jerky to cool at room temperature. Transfer to a covered container that allows a bit of airflow and store in a cool, dark place for up to 6 weeks.

CONTINUED

Worcestershire sauce, named for Worcester, England, its original place of manufacture, is a curiously complex blend of ingredients that, simmered together, creates a unique, umami-rich sauce that is more than the sum of its parts. Store-bought Worcestershire sauce, which tends to be loaded with sweeteners and preservatives, can't compete in flavor with this homemade version. It's a splendid seasoning for jerky and a great marinade for grilled meats, and a dash in your glass will enliven your next Bloody Mary.

WORCESTERSHIRE SAUCE

MAKES ABOUT 1½ CUPS (360 ML)

1 tablespoon olive oil

1 yellow onion, sliced

1 jalapeño chile, sliced into rounds

2 cloves garlic, crushed

½ teaspoon black peppercorns

2 anchovy fillets, rinsed

3 whole cloves

1 teaspoon fine sea salt

½ lemon, skin and pith removed

¾ cup (250 g) molasses

¼ cup (50 g) sugar

¾ cup (180 ml) white wine vinegar

¾ cup (180 ml) water

¼ cup (50 g) freshly grated horseradish root

Heat the olive oil in a saucepan over medium heat. Add the onion, jalapeño, and garlic and cook, stirring frequently, until caramelized, about 15 minutes. Add the peppercorns, anchovies, cloves, salt, lemon, molasses, sugar, vinegar, water, and horseradish to the pan and bring to a boil. Lower the heat and simmer gently, stirring from time to time, until the mixture is reduced by about one-third, about 1½ hours. Strain the liquid into a clean glass jar.

Allow the sauce to cool, then cover and refrigerate for up to 3 months.

Moo dat diow is a Thai specialty, often served as an appetizer or sold as a snack by street-food vendors. The little strips of pork are tossed in a simple, garlicky marinade, then hung to dry in the hot Thai sun. Traditionally, the lightly dried meat is then deep-fried or grilled, but in a rare break with tradition, we've found that we prefer these tasty pork morsels when dried in the dehydrator and eaten as is.

This recipe uses not the leaves of the cilantro plant but rather the thin, white roots, which have a more delicate, subtle flavor than the leaves and don't discolor when dried. Look for bunches of cilantro with the roots still attached in Asian grocery stores. Be sure to wash the roots well to remove any dirt that may still be clinging to them. If cilantro roots are unavailable, you can substitute the stems.

THAI-STYLE PORK JERKY

MAKES ABOUT 1 POUND (450 G)

4 cloves garlic

1 teaspoon fine sea salt

¼ cup (17 g) chopped fresh cilantro roots and/or stems

3 tablespoons fish sauce

¼ cup (60 ml) soy sauce

2 teaspoons white peppercorns, lightly toasted and finely ground

2 tablespoons brown sugar

2 pounds (910 g) trimmed pork sirloin or loin, cut into strips ½ inch (12 mm) in diameter and 4 to 5 inches (10 to 12 cm) long

Using a mortar and pestle, pound the garlic and salt to make a paste. Add the cilantro root and/or stems and continue to pound to a coarse paste.

In a shallow bowl or container, combine the garlic-cilantro paste, the fish sauce, soy sauce, white pepper, and sugar. Add the pork strips and, using your hands, mix well to evenly coat the strips. Cover and refrigerate for at least 1 day or up to 2 days.

When you are ready to dry the pork, remove the meat from the refrigerator. Place the strips on the racks of your dehydrator, keeping them straight and making sure that no strips are overlapping or touching. Set the temperature to 145°F (63°C). Insert the racks into the dehydrator, leaving as much space as possible between them. Dehydrate for about 2 hours, until the strips are firm but still pliable, rotating the racks front to back halfway through to ensure even drying.

Allow the jerky to cool at room temperature. Transfer to a covered container that allows a bit of airflow and store in a cool, dark place for up to 3 weeks.

Good, grass-fed bison is naturally lean and high in protein and an excellent choice for anyone seeking a healthier meat option. But you don't have to be on a health kick to appreciate the bright herbal flavors of this jerky. Juniper, bay, and sage are natural complements to sweet, grassy-tasting bison meat.

In addition to being lean, the muscle fibers of bison can be quite dense. Be sure to cut the bison in thin, even slices against the grain and take care not to overdry the meat.

PRAIRIE BISON

MAKES ABOUT 1 POUND (450 G)

1 clove garlic

1 tablespoon plus 1 teaspoon fine sea salt

1 bay leaf, crumbled

1 juniper berry

1 tablespoon dried sage

1 teaspoon black peppercorns

2 pounds (910 g) trimmed bison top round, sliced ⅛ to ¼ inch (3 to 6 mm) thick against the grain

2 teaspoons brown sugar

Using a mortar and pestle, pound the garlic with the salt to form a paste. Combine the bay leaf, juniper berry, sage, and peppercorns in a spice grinder and pulverize until finely ground.

Place the sliced bison in a shallow bowl or container. Massage the garlic paste into the meat, then season with the ground spices and the brown sugar. Using your hands, mix well to evenly coat the slices. Cover and refrigerate for at least 3 hours or up to overnight.

When you are ready to dry the bison, remove the meat from the refrigerator. Place the slices on the racks of your dehydrator, making sure that no slices are overlapping. Set the temperature to 145°F (63°C). Insert the racks into the dehydrator, leaving as much space as possible between them. Dehydrate for about 2 hours, until the slices are firm but still pliable, rotating the racks front to back halfway through to ensure even drying.

Allow the jerky to cool at room temperature. Transfer to a covered container that allows a bit of airflow and store in a cool, dark place for up to 6 weeks.

True teriyaki sauce is quite unlike the gloppy bottled versions that line supermarket shelves. *Teri* is the Japanese word for "luster" and *yaki* means "grilled." Fresh off the grill (or out of the dehydrator), this lustrous pork jerky, with its bright, vibrant flavors, will blow away any sticky-sweet notions you may have about teriyaki. We tend to prefer pork for this jerky, but you can substitute beef or bison.

PORK TERIYAKI

MAKES ABOUT 1 POUND (450 G)

2 teaspoons fine sea salt

½ cup (120 ml) soy sauce

4 tablespoons (85 g) honey

2 tablespoons mirin

6 tablespoons (90 ml) sake

1 teaspoon freshly ground white pepper

4 cloves garlic, lightly crushed

1 tablespoon peeled and grated fresh ginger

2 pounds (910 g) trimmed pork sirloin, sliced ⅛ to ¼ inch (3 to 6 mm) thick against the grain

In a small bowl, whisk together the salt, ¼ cup (60 ml) of the soy sauce, 2 tablespoons of the honey, the mirin, and 2 tablespoons of the sake. Stir in the white pepper, garlic, and ginger.

Place the sliced pork in a shallow bowl or container, then pour the soy sauce mixture over the meat. Using your hands, mix well to evenly coat the slices. Cover and refrigerate for at least 3 hours or up to overnight.

When you are ready to dry the meat, remove the pork from the refrigerator. To make a glaze, in a small bowl, whisk together the remaining ¼ cup (60 ml) soy sauce, the remaining 2 tablespoons honey, and the remaining 4 tablespoons (60 ml) sake.

Place the slices on the racks of your dehydrator, making sure that no slices are overlapping. Using a pastry brush, baste the top of each slice with the glaze. Set the temperature to 145°F (63°C). Insert the racks into the dehydrator, leaving as much space as possible between them. Dehydrate for about 2 hours, until the slices are firm but still pliable, rotating the racks front to back halfway through to ensure even drying.

Alternatively, you can use a smoker or grill. Place the slices on the racks, making sure that no slices are overlapping. Using a pastry brush, baste the top of each slice with the glaze. Place the racks into the smoker or grill. You want to keep the temperature in the smoker or grill between 140°F and 160°F (60°C and 65°C). Dry the jerky for 1½ to 2 hours, until the slices are firm but still pliable, rotating the pieces frequently to ensure even drying.

Allow the jerky to cool at room temperature. Transfer to a covered container that allows a bit of airflow and store in a cool, dark place for up to 3 weeks.

This is our standard fare and the meaty staple we've produced daily at The Fatted Calf Charcuterie for the last fifteen years. In our shop, this jerky is nearly always being trimmed, thinly sliced, marinated in its boozy slurry, or being prepared for cold smoking and drying. But the best part of the day, even after all these years, is when the timer signals the end of the last drying cycle, and the finished jerky, with its alluring scent, emerges from the dehydrator, warm and delicious. It's hard to resist!

BOURBON AND MOLASSES SMOKED BEEF JERKY

MAKES ABOUT 1 POUND (450 G)

1 tablespoon plus 1 teaspoon fine sea salt

¼ cup (60 ml) bourbon

2 tablespoons blackstrap molasses

½ teaspoon freshly ground black pepper

2 pounds (910 g) trimmed beef bottom round, sliced ⅛ to ¼ inch (3 to 6 mm) thick against the grain

In a small bowl, whisk together the salt and bourbon until the salt is completely dissolved, then stir in the molasses and pepper and mix well.

Place the sliced beef in a shallow bowl or container. Pour the bourbon mixture over the meat. Using your hands, mix well to evenly coat the slices. Cover and refrigerate for at least 3 hours or up to overnight.

When you are ready to smoke the beef, remove the meat from the refrigerator. Fit a rimmed baking sheet with a wire rack and place the beef slices on the rack. You can shingle the meat so the slices overlap, but make sure it is no more than 2 slices deep so all of the meat is exposed to the smoke. Place the baking sheet in the smoker and cold smoke for 1 hour (see page 24). Alternatively, if you prefer your jerky without the smoky flavor or if you do not have access to a smoker, you can skip this step and proceed to the next.

Set the temperature of the dehydrator to 145°F (63°C). Place the slices of beef on the dehydrator racks, making sure that no slices are overlapping. Insert the racks into the dehydrator, leaving as much space as possible between them. Dehydrate for about 2½ hours, until the slices are firm but still pliable, rotating the racks front to back halfway through to ensure even drying.

Allow the jerky to cool at room temperature. Transfer to a covered container that allows a bit of airflow and store in a cool, dark place for up to 5 weeks.

This capricious pork jerky is seasoned with a blend of pastoral herbs, with the lavender adding a certain je ne sais quoi. It begs to be enjoyed in the great outdoors, perhaps accompanied by a bottle of luscious rosé, and will become an instant favorite for your picnic basket.

This jerky, in particular, benefits from at least one full day of marinating to allow the herbs to permeate the pork. We prefer to dry this jerky in the dehydrator without the addition of smoke, to allow the bright, clean flavors to shine.

PORK PIQUE-NIQUE

MAKES ABOUT 1 POUND (450 G)

2 cloves garlic

1 tablespoon plus 1 teaspoon fine sea salt

½ teaspoon black peppercorns

¼ teaspoon white peppercorns

1 fresh or dried lavender bud

2 pounds (910 g) trimmed pork sirloin, cut into strips ½ inch (12 mm) in diameter

½ bay leaf

A few sprigs each of fresh rosemary, oregano, and thyme

Using a mortar and pestle, pound the garlic with 1 teaspoon of the salt to form a paste. Using a spice grinder, grind together the black and white peppercorns. Lightly bruise the lavender bud.

Place the pork strips in a shallow bowl or container. Massage the garlic paste into the meat, then season with the ground pepper. Add the lavender, bay leaf, and herb sprigs. Using your hands, mix well to evenly coat the slices. Cover and refrigerate for at least 1 day or up to 2 days.

When you are ready to dry the pork, remove the meat from the refrigerator. Place the strips on the racks of your dehydrator, keeping them straight and making sure that no strips are overlapping or touching. Set the temperature to 145°F (63°C). Insert the racks into the dehydrator, leaving as much space as possible between them. Dehydrate for about 2½ hours, until the strips are firm but still pliable, rotating the racks front to back halfway through to ensure even drying.

Allow the jerky to cool at room temperature. Transfer to a covered container that allows a bit of airflow and store in a cool, dark place for up to 4 weeks.

In Korea, beef jerky, known as *yukpo*, is typically given as a ceremonial wedding gift. The happy marriage of pear juice, soy, honey, and *gochugaru* (Korean chile flakes) give this beef jerky a perfect salty, tangy, sweet, and mildly spicy balance. For the special occasion, we've dressed this jerky with a gorgeous veil of crunchy sesame seeds, making it as beautiful to behold as it is fun to eat.

THE WEDDING PRESENT

**MAKES ABOUT 1 POUND
(450 G)**

½ cup (120 ml) pear or
apple juice

3 tablespoons soy sauce

3 tablespoons honey

3 tablespoons gochugaru

1 tablespoon fine sea salt

2 pounds (910 g) trimmed
beef bottom round, sliced
⅛ to ¼ inch (3 to 6 mm) thick
across the grain

½ cup (80 g) sesame seeds,
toasted

In a large bowl, whisk together the pear juice, soy sauce, honey, gochugaru, and salt. Place the sliced beef in the bowl with the marinade. Using your hands, mix well to evenly coat the slices. Cover and refrigerate for at least 3 hours or up to overnight.

When you are ready to dry the beef, remove the meat from the refrigerator. Spread the sesame seeds out on a plate. Dredge one side of each meat slice in the sesame seeds to coat, then place the slices, seed-side up, onto the racks of your dehydrator, making sure that no slices are overlapping. Set the temperature to 145°F (63°C). Insert the racks into the dehydrator, leaving as much space as possible between them. Dehydrate for about 2 hours, until the slices are firm but still pliable, rotating the racks front to back halfway through to ensure even drying.

Allow the jerky to cool at room temperature. Transfer to a covered container that allows a bit of airflow and store in a cool, dark place for up to 4 weeks.

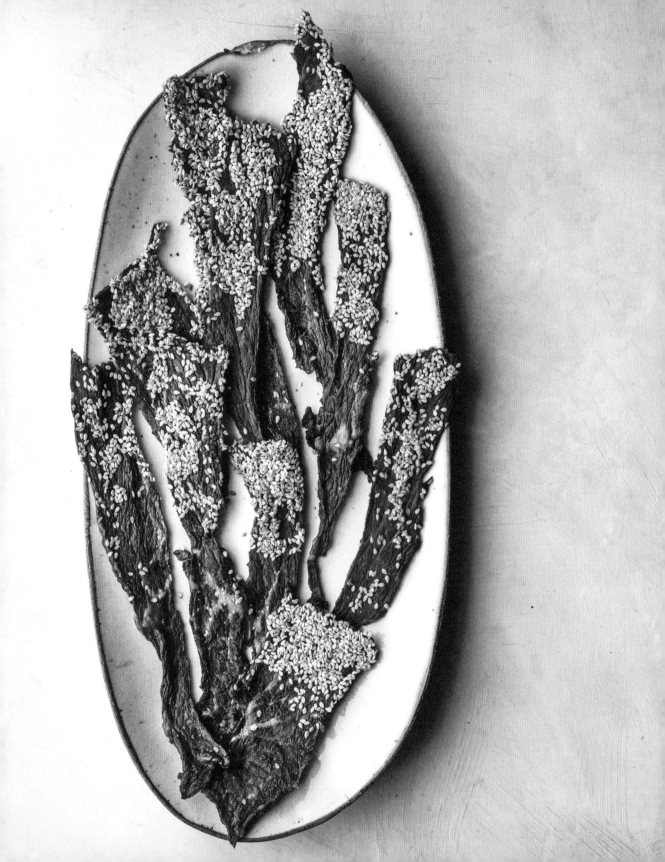

SOME LIKE IT HOT

Eating freshly dried jerky straight from the smoker or out of the dehydrator is a special treat. Warm jerky has that melt-in-your-mouth quality that's hard to beat. When the jerky cools, the texture often becomes more rigid, and as the jerky ages, it can become more brittle and the flavors more muted. But you can perk up your jerky by quickly reheating it. Just place a few slices of jerky on a baking sheet and put it in a 325°F (165°C) oven for about 10 minutes to heat through.

This dried meat specialty hails from the neighboring Italian regions of Lazio and Umbria. *Coppiette*, or "little couples," are so named because the long strips of meat were customarily hung to dry in pairs. Although traditionally made from the sinewy hind quarters of "retired" farm animals such as donkeys and goats, the *coppiette* you typically find in *salumerie* today are made mainly with pork. We were happily surprised to come across this herbaceous wild boar version of *coppiette* on a recent trip to Rome. Enjoy as part of an antipasto course with a glass of earthy red wine.

WILD BOAR COPPIETTE

MAKES ABOUT 1 POUND (450 G)

3 cloves garlic, lightly crushed

1 tablespoon plus 1 teaspoon salt

1 bay leaf

1 juniper berry

2 teaspoons black peppercorns

2 pounds (910 g) trimmed wild boar or pork sirloin, cut into strips ½ inch (12 mm) in diameter

1 sprig fresh rosemary

⅓ cup (75 ml) red wine

Using a mortar and pestle, pound the garlic with the salt to form a paste. Combine the bay leaf, juniper berry, and peppercorns in a spice grinder and pulverize until finely ground.

Place the boar strips in a shallow bowl or container. Massage the garlic paste into the meat, then season with the ground spices. Add the rosemary sprig and, using your hands, mix well to evenly coat the strips. Cover and refrigerate for at least 3 hours or up to overnight.

When you are ready to dry the boar, remove the meat from the refrigerator. Place the strips on the racks of your dehydrator, keeping them straight and making sure that no strips are overlapping or touching. Set the temperature to 145°F (63°C). Insert the racks into the dehydrator, leaving as much space as possible between them. Dehydrate for about 2 hours, until the strips are firm but still pliable, rotating the racks front to back halfway through to ensure even drying.

Allow the *coppiette* to cool at room temperature. Transfer to a covered container that allows a bit of airflow and store in a cool, dark place for up to 6 weeks.

CHAPTER TWO

FIERY AND
FULL-FLAVORED
JERKY

Ganba is a boldly flavored dried-meat specialty from China's Yunnan Province. The list of ingredients is short and the process relatively simple, but this smoky beef seasoned with both chile and mouth-numbing Szechuan peppercorns is not for amateur jerky lovers.

Rather than being simply eaten out of hand, *ganba* is a pantry staple for cooking. It is customarily combined with other ingredients that temper its intensity. Shredded or pounded, it can be simmered in soups or stir-fried with potatoes. In Gingery Cabbage Slaw with Smoky Beef and Herbs (page 109), it's pounded into shreds, then mixed with herbs and chiles.

GANBA

MAKES ABOUT 1 POUND (450 G)

1 teaspoon Szechuan peppercorns

2 pounds (910 g) trimmed beef bottom round, cut into strips ½ inch (12 mm) in diameter and 4 to 5 inches (10 to 12 cm) long

1 tablespoon plus 1 teaspoon fine sea salt

2 teaspoons chile flakes

In a dry skillet over medium heat, toast the Szechuan peppercorns until fragrant. Allow to cool to room temperature. Using a spice grinder, pulverize the peppercorns to a fine powder.

Place the beef strips in a shallow bowl or container. Season with the salt, chile flakes, and ground Szechuan peppercorns. Using your hands, mix well to evenly coat the strips. Cover and refrigerate for at least 3 hours or up to overnight.

When you are ready to smoke the beef, remove the meat from the refrigerator. Prepare your grill or smoker. You want to keep the temperature between 140°F and 160°F (60°C and 65°C). Fit a rimmed baking sheet with a wire rack. Place the strips on the rack, keeping them straight and making sure that no strips are overlapping or touching. Alternatively, skewer the meat for smoking. Place the beef in the smoker or on the grill to smoke for about 1½ hours, checking the progress and rotating every 15 minutes or so, until the strips are firm and dry but still pliable.

Allow the *ganba* to cool to room temperature. Transfer to a covered container that allows a bit of airflow and store in a cool, dark place for up to 6 weeks.

Citrusy lemongrass predominates in *thit bo kho*, a Vietnamese-style beef jerky. A native of Vietnam that flourishes in the tropical climate, lemongrass is multipurpose. In addition to perfuming the jerky with its enticing scent, it also has antifungal properties that help preserve the beef.

Thit bo kho can be eaten on its own or as part of a meal. Try shredding the jerky and serving it over sticky rice or adding it to a green papaya salad.

LEMONGRASS BEEF

MAKES ABOUT 1 POUND (450 G)

2 medium lemongrass stalks

3 tablespoons fish sauce

2 tablespoons honey

1 tablespoon oyster sauce

2 green onions, finely chopped

1 clove garlic, minced

2 pounds (910 g) trimmed beef bottom round, sliced ⅛ to ¼ inch (3 to 6 mm) thick against the grain

2 teaspoons fine sea salt

1 tablespoon ground turmeric

1 tablespoon five-spice powder

1 tablespoon chile flakes

Trim away the tough base and woody top part of the lemongrass stalks. Peel away any loose outer layers, leaving just the smooth, tender center. Using a heavy chef's knife or cleaver, slice each stalk in half lengthwise, then chop finely.

In a small bowl, stir together the fish sauce, honey, oyster sauce, lemongrass, onions, and garlic.

Place the sliced beef in a shallow bowl or container. Season with the salt, turmeric, five-spice powder, and chile flakes and toss to coat. Pour the fish sauce mixture over the beef and, using your hands, mix well to evenly coat the slices. Cover and refrigerate overnight.

When you are ready to dry the beef, remove the meat from the refrigerator. Lay the slices on the racks of your dehydrator, making sure that no slices are overlapping. Set the temperature to 145°F (63°C). Insert the racks into the dehydrator, leaving as much space as possible between them. Dehydrate for about 2½ hours, until the slices are firm but still pliable, rotating the racks front to back halfway through to ensure even drying.

Allow the *bo kho* to cool at room temperature. Transfer to a covered container that allows a bit of airflow and store in a cool, dark place for up to 6 weeks.

Puckery tamarind and fragrant kaffir lime leaf give this beef jerky an alluring and exotic appeal. In Indonesia and Malaysia, *dendeng balado* is nearly always lightly air-dried and then deep-fried or stir-fried. But we favor the intensity of this version that's fully dried in the dehydrator.

DENDENG BALADO

MAKES ABOUT 1 POUND (450 G)

1 tablespoon coriander seed

2 teaspoons black peppercorns

1 tablespoon fine sea salt

2 tablespoons chopped shallot

3 cloves garlic, roughly chopped

3 red Thai chiles, stemmed and chopped

2 kaffir lime leaves, roughly chopped

2 tablespoons palm sugar or brown sugar

⅛ teaspoon ground cinnamon

¼ teaspoon freshly grated nutmeg

3 tablespoons kecap manis (Indonesian sweet soy sauce)

2 tablespoons tamarind paste dissolved in 2 tablespoons hot water

2 pounds (910 g) trimmed beef bottom round, sliced ⅛ to ¼ inch (3 to 6 mm) thick against the grain

In a dry skillet over low heat, toast the coriander and peppercorns until fragrant. Allow to cool to room temperature. Using a mortar and pestle, coarsely grind the toasted spices. Add the salt, shallot, garlic, chiles, and lime leaves and pound to a smooth paste. Add the sugar, cinnamon, nutmeg, *kecap manis*, and tamarind and mix well.

Place the sliced beef in a shallow bowl or container. Pour the marinade over the beef. Using your hands, mix well to evenly coat the slices. Cover and refrigerate for at least 3 hours or up to overnight.

When you are ready to dry the beef, remove the meat from the refrigerator. Place the slices on the racks of your dehydrator, making sure that no slices are overlapping. Set the temperature to 145°F (63°C). Insert the racks into the dehydrator, leaving as much space as possible between them. Dehydrate for about 2½ hours, until the slices are firm but still pliable, rotating the racks front to back halfway through to ensure even drying.

Allow the *dendeng balado* to cool at room temperature. Transfer to a covered container that allows a bit of airflow and store in a cool, dark place for up to 6 weeks.

We were lucky to have visited the small town of Norcia, tucked into the southeastern corner of the Italian region of Umbria, in the spring of 2012, before it was rocked by devastating earthquakes in 2016. This picture-perfect town was well-known for its Renaissance architecture and even more famous for its devotion and exultation of all things swine related. Norcia was a veritable fantasyland for cured-meat aficionados, a place worthy of pilgrimage. At the dozen or more *salumerie* we visited, prosciutti and salami hung from every hook, every rafter, every doorway and spilled out into the stone streets in baskets and wine crates. In Norcia we found the most enticing *coppiette* we had ever seen: long, elegant strips resembling *grissini*, traditional Piemontese breadsticks, that were cut from pork loin and laden with fennel and chile.

Pork loin is a bit extravagant compared with some other cuts of meat used for jerky, but since it is quite lean, it requires very little trimming and provides a good yield. These *coppiette* are best dried in a dehydrator or oven, as smoke can overshadow the delicate flavors of the fennel pollen and white wine.

COPPIETTE DI NORCIA

MAKES ABOUT 1 POUND (450 G)

2 pounds (910 g) trimmed pork loin, cut into strips ½ inch (12 mm) in diameter and 8 to 10 inches (20 to 25 cm) long

1 tablespoon plus 1 teaspoon fine sea salt

1½ teaspoons chile flakes

1 teaspoon fennel pollen

1 teaspoon unsmoked Spanish paprika

2 tablespoons dry white wine

Place the pork strips in a shallow bowl or container. Season with the salt, then add the chile flakes, fennel pollen, paprika, and wine. Using your hands, mix well to evenly coat the strips. Cover and refrigerate for at least 3 hours or up to overnight.

When you are ready to dry the pork, remove the meat from the refrigerator. Place the strips on the racks of your dehydrator, keeping them straight and making sure that no strips are overlapping or touching. Set the temperature to 145°F (63°C). Insert the racks into the dehydrator, leaving as much space as possible between them. Dehydrate for about 2½ hours, until the strips are firm but still pliable, rotating the racks front to back halfway through to ensure even drying.

Allow the *coppiette* to cool at room temperature. Transfer to a covered container that allows a bit of airflow and store in a cool, dark place for up to 4 weeks.

EAT JERKY LIKE AN ITALIAN

The innkeepers of Agriturismo Pettino, located in a tiny mountain village in Umbria, were generous and welcoming, heaping our dinner plates each night with black truffles, local lamb, and fresh pasta. When they learned of our intent to visit the not-so-nearby town of (*bella*!) Norcia, they waxed rhapsodic about the salami, the prosciutti, and especially the delicious *coppiette* one could procure there. Delighted for the opportunity to reciprocate their kindness, when we arrived in Norcia, we stocked up on *coppiette*, some of which we happily munched straight from the bag during the long ride back up the mountainside. We gifted the remaining *coppiette* to our hosts. Amid a profusion of *grazie mille*, the table was set with plates, knives, forks, napkins, and a cruet of olive oil. The *coppiette* were served with olive oil drizzled on top, and we watched in amazement, hiding our greasy fingers still stained red with chile, as they dug in with knife and fork.

Who doesn't love a solidly stacked pastrami sandwich outfitted with all the trimmings? But demolishing one whole can be coma inducing. Here is a portable, pastrami-spiced jerky to satisfy those pesky cravings when you just can't commit to the whole sandwich.

POCKET PASTRAMI

MAKES ABOUT 1 POUND (450 G)

1 tablespoon coriander seed

1½ teaspoons black peppercorns

¼ teaspoon cumin seed

1½ teaspoons yellow mustard seed

2 pounds (910 g) well-trimmed beef brisket, sliced ⅛ to ¼ inch (3 to 6 mm) thick against the grain

1 tablespoon plus 1½ teaspoon fine sea salt

1 tablespoon plus 1 teaspoon brown sugar

1 tablespoon unsmoked Spanish paprika

¼ teaspoon cayenne

In a dry skillet over low heat, toast the coriander, peppercorns, cumin, and mustard until fragrant. Allow to cool to room temperature. Using a spice grinder, pulverize to a fine powder.

Place the sliced beef in a shallow bowl or container. Season with the salt, then add the ground spices, the brown sugar, paprika, and cayenne. Using your hands, mix well to evenly coat the slices. Let stand at room temperature for 20 minutes to allow the sugar and salt to dissolve, then mix again. Cover and refrigerate for at least 3 hours or up to overnight.

When you are ready to dry the beef, remove the meat from the refrigerator. Place the slices on the racks of your dehydrator, making sure that no slices are overlapping. Set the temperature to 145°F (63°C). Insert the racks into the dehydrator, leaving as much space as possible between them. Dehydrate for about 2½ hours, until the slices are firm but still pliable, rotating the racks front to back halfway through to ensure even drying.

Allow the pastrami jerky to cool at room temperature. Transfer to a covered container that allows a bit of airflow and store in a cool, dark place for up to 4 weeks.

Cecina, sometimes called *tasajo*, is thin sheets of dried beef or pork. Common throughout Mexico, *cecina* can be fully dried and eaten as is, or lightly dried and finished on the grill to make tacos and Enfrijoladas con Cecina (page 97).

Pork pairs especially well with this piquant *adobada* marinade made with chiles, vinegar, and Mexican oregano, but you can also try this recipe with beef or even goat leg or loin.

CECINA ADOBADA

MAKES ABOUT 1 POUND
(450 G) FULLY DRIED OR
ABOUT 1½ POUNDS (680 G)
LIGHTLY DRIED

2 guajillo chiles

2 ancho chiles

1 teaspoon black peppercorns

1 teaspoon cumin seed

2 whole cloves

2 allspice berries

3 cloves garlic, unpeeled

1 tablespoon plus 1 teaspoon
fine sea salt

⅛ teaspoon ground cinnamon

3 tablespoons plantain vinegar
or other fruity vinegar

1 teaspoon dried Mexican
oregano, crumbled

2 pounds (910 g) trimmed
pork sirloin, sliced ⅛ to ¼ inch
(3 to 6 mm) thick against
the grain

In a dry skillet over medium heat, toast the chiles for roughly 30 seconds per side. Allow to cool to room temperature. Stem and seed the chiles. In the same skillet over medium heat, toast the peppercorns, cumin, cloves, and allspice until fragrant. Allow to cool to room temperature. Combine the toasted chiles and spices in a spice grinder and pulverize to a fine powder.

Return the skillet to medium-low heat, add the garlic cloves, and toast, occasionally shaking the pan, until the skins are spotty brown and the garlic is soft, about 5 minutes. Allow to cool, then peel. Using a mortar and pestle, pound the garlic with the salt to form a paste. Add the ground chile-spice mixture, the cinnamon, vinegar, and oregano and mix to blend.

Place the sliced pork in a shallow bowl or container. Add the marinade and, using your hands, mix well to evenly coat the slices. Cover and refrigerate for at least 3 hours or up to overnight.

When you are ready to dry the pork, remove the meat from the refrigerator. Place the slices on the racks of your dehydrator, making sure that no slices are overlapping. Set the temperature to 145°F (63°C). Insert the racks into the dehydrator, leaving as much space as possible between them. Dehydrate for about 2½ hours, until the slices are firm but still pliable, rotating the racks front to back halfway through to ensure even drying. (Alternatively, if you will be cooking the *cecina*, dehydrate for just 30 minutes, then grill or pan fry as desired.)

Allow the *cecina* to cool at room temperature. Transfer to a covered container that allows a bit of airflow and store in a cool, dark place for up to 3 weeks.

Gueddid is the traditional spiced meat of Morocco, where it is dried outdoors in the hot summer sun. Generally, *gueddid* is thoroughly dried for preservation, to be used later in bean dishes, couscous, and stews, but this tantalizingly spiced jerky also makes a tasty anytime snack. We favor lean, mild goat meat for this jerky, but you can also prepare *gueddid* with beef bottom round or lamb leg.

GOAT GUEDDID

MAKES ABOUT 1 POUND (450 G)

2 tablespoons coriander seed

2 tablespoons cumin seed

2 teaspoons caraway seed

2 teaspoons fennel seed

2 teaspoons black peppercorns

5 cloves garlic

1 tablespoon plus 1 teaspoon fine sea salt

¼ cup (60 ml) olive oil

3 tablespoons red wine vinegar

3 tablespoons unsmoked Spanish paprika

1 tablespoon cayenne

1 teaspoon ground turmeric

2 pounds (910 g) trimmed goat loin or leg, beef bottom round, or lamb leg, sliced ⅛ to ¼ inch (3 to 6 mm) thick against the grain

In a dry skillet over medium heat, toast the coriander, cumin, caraway, fennel, and peppercorns until fragrant. Allow to cool to room temperature. Using a spice grinder, pulverize the spices to a fine powder.

Using a mortar and pestle, pound together the garlic and salt to form a paste. Stir in the ground spices, the olive oil, vinegar, paprika, cayenne, and turmeric.

Place the sliced meat in a shallow bowl or container. Add the garlic-spice mixture and, using your hands, mix well to evenly coat the slices. Cover and refrigerate for at least 3 hours or up to overnight.

When you are ready to dry the goat, remove the meat from the refrigerator. Place the slices on the racks of your dehydrator, making sure that no slices are overlapping. Set the temperature to 145°F (63°C). Insert the racks into the dehydrator, leaving as much space as possible between them. Dehydrate for about 2 hours, until the slices are firm but still pliable, rotating the racks front to back halfway through to ensure even drying.

Alternatively, you can sun-dry the meat (see page 18) for 24 to 48 hours.

Allow the *gueddid* to cool at room temperature. Transfer to a covered container that allows a bit of airflow and store in a cool, dark place for up to 4 weeks.

The spicy, tangy, sweetness of fermented chile and miso combined with the naturally buttery flavor of the pork ping-pongs around the taste buds, triggering those happy sensory neurons that will have you reaching for another piece of this jerky almost immediately. If you like, you can substitute beef for the pork.

PORK WITH FERMENTED CHILE AND MISO SAUCE

MAKES ABOUT 1 POUND (450 G)

2 pounds (910 g) trimmed pork sirloin, sliced ⅛ to ¼ inch (3 to 6 mm) thick

1 tablespoon fine sea salt

6 tablespoons (90 ml) Fermented Chile and Miso Sauce (page 66)

Place the sliced pork in a shallow bowl or container. Season with the salt, then add the sauce. Using your hands, mix well to evenly coat the slices. Cover and refrigerate for at least 3 hours or up to overnight.

When you are ready to dry the meat, remove the pork from the refrigerator. Place the slices on the racks of your dehydrator, making sure that no slices are overlapping. Set the temperature to 145°F (63°C). Insert the racks into the dehydrator, leaving as much space as possible between them. Dehydrate for about 2½ hours, until the slices are firm but still pliable, rotating the racks front to back halfway through to ensure even drying.

Allow the jerky to cool at room temperature. Transfer to a covered container that allows a bit of airflow and store in a cool, dark place for up to 4 weeks.

CONTINUED

QUANTA

page 111.

Provocatively spiced *quanta* (somet
is an Ethiopian favorite that is eate
as an ingredient in hearty dishes su
page 111. Don't be intimidated by
specialty. The finished jerky is spicy

**MAKES ABOUT 1 POUND
(450 G)**

Seeds from 2 cardamom pods

¼ teaspoon fenugreek seed

¼ teaspoon black peppercorns

½ teaspoon cumin seed

¼ teaspoon coriander seed

¼ teaspoon nigella seed

2 cloves garlic

1 tablespoon plus 1 teaspoon
fine sea salt

6 dried bird's-eye chiles

1 teaspoon peeled and grated
fresh ginger

2 pounds (910 g) trimmed
beef bottom round, sliced
⅛ to ¼ inch (3 to 6 mm) thick
against the grain

¼ teaspoon ground turmeric

⅛ teaspoon freshly grated
nutmeg

In a dry skillet over low heat, toast
peppercorns, cumin, coriander, an
to cool to room temperature. Usin
the spices to a powder.

Using a mortar and pestle, pound t
chiles and ginger and continue pou

Place the sliced beef in a shallow b
the garlic-chile paste into the mea
mixture, the turmeric, and the nut
well to evenly coat the slices. Cove
3 hours or up to overnight.

When you are ready to dry the bee
refrigerator. Place the slices on the
making sure that no slices are ove
to 145°F (63°C). Insert the racks i
as much space as possible between
2½ hours, until the slices are firm
racks front to back halfway throug

Allow the *quanta* to cool at room te
container that allows a bit of airflow
for up to 6 weeks.

We grow a variety of chiles in our li[...]
time, we get busy drying chiles, ca[...]
preparing funky fermented concoct[...]
miso paste. The fermenting proces[...]
with a pleasant tanginess. You can [...]
meats for grilling or roasting, as a [...]
or as a condiment for sandwiches [...]

FERMENTED CHILE AND MISO SAUCE

**MAKES ABOUT 4 CUPS
(960 ML)**

3 to 4 cups (525 to 700 g)
fresh spicy red chiles
(such as jalapeño, serrano,
or Thai), stemmed

1 cup (240 ml) water

½ cup (170 g) honey

¾ cup (220 g) red miso

1 tablespoon fine sea salt

1 teaspoon sake

1 teaspoon rice vinegar

Place the chiles in the workbowl of[...]
to a coarse paste, about 45 secon[...]

Combine the water and honey in [...]
simmer over medium heat. Cook u[...]
half, then stir in the miso. Lower th[...]
stirring frequently, for an additiona[...]
temperature, then mix in the chile [...]

Pour the mixture into a 2-quart (2-[...]
Cover the jar with cheesecloth or le[...]
mixture can breathe, then place in [...]
cabinet or above your refrigerator. [...]
1 week. The finished mixture will h[...]
overripe scent and will have thicke[...]
and rice vinegar, then pour into a [...]
The sauce will keep in the refrigere[...]

We've always enjoyed the curious Italian herbal distillates known as *amari* in cocktails or as post-feast digestives, but lately we've been pouring splashes into sauces and marinades with delicious results. These beguiling elixirs add an elusive flavor, a delicate herbal finish that leaves you musing. An amaro, combined with allspice, chile, and orange zest make these little pork bites sophisticated enough to serve with cocktails at your next soirée.

THE BITTER PIG

MAKES ABOUT 1 POUND (450 G)

2 teaspoons anise seed

4 allspice berries

2 pounds (910 g) trimmed pork sirloin or loin, cut into strips ½ inch (12 mm) in diameter and 3 to 4 inches (7.5 to 10 cm) long

1 tablespoon plus 1 teaspoon fine sea salt

1 tablespoon chile flakes

½ teaspoon grated and finely chopped orange zest

2 tablespoons amaro (such as Averna or Meletti)

In a dry skillet over low heat, toast the anise and allspice until fragrant. Allow to cool to room temperature. Using a spice grinder, pulverize the spices to a fine powder.

Place the pork strips in a shallow bowl or container. Season with the salt, then add the ground spices, the chile flakes, orange zest, and amaro. Using your hands, mix well to evenly coat the strips. Cover and refrigerate for at least 3 hours or up to overnight.

When you are ready to dry the pork, remove the meat from the refrigerator. Place the strips on the racks of your dehydrator, making sure that no strips are overlapping or touching. Set the temperature to 145°F (63°C). Insert the racks into the dehydrator, leaving as much space as possible between them. Dehydrate for 2½ hours, until the strips are firm but still pliable, rotating the racks front to back halfway through to ensure even drying.

Allow the jerky to cool at room temperature. Transfer to a covered container that allows a bit of airflow and store in a cool, dark place for up to 4 weeks.

CHAPTER THREE

JERKY'S KIN

We are lucky to have a good number of friends who are avid mushroom hunters and who provide us access to plenty of freshly foraged wild mushrooms. But we find dried wild mushrooms, which are readily available, to be nearly as good for many dishes, including this ground pork and porcini specialty. If you love mushrooms as much as you love jerky, this recipe is for you. Pack a few pieces for your next walk in the woods or enjoy as a nibble with a glass of robust red wine.

PORK AND PORCINI BITES

MAKES ABOUT 1½ POUNDS (680 G)

½ ounce (15 g) dried porcini or other dried wild mushrooms

2 large shallots, minced

2 tablespoons olive oil

¾ cup (180 ml) red wine

2 pounds (910 g) finely ground lean pork

1 tablespoon plus 1 teaspoon fine sea salt

1 teaspoon freshly ground black pepper

1 tablespoon chopped fresh thyme

Put the mushrooms in a bowl, add cold water to cover them by about 1 inch (2.5 cm), and let rehydrate at room temperature for at least 3 hours or up to overnight. Using your hands or a slotted spoon, gently remove the mushrooms from their soaking liquid, leaving any grit in the bottom of the bowl. Strain the soaking liquid through a fine-mesh sieve and set aside. Pat the mushrooms dry and chop finely.

In a small sauté pan over low heat, cook the shallots in the olive oil, stirring occasionally, until translucent, about 10 minutes. Add the mushrooms and continue to cook, stirring occasionally, for an additional 5 minutes. Pour in the strained mushroom liquid and the wine. Bring to a gentle simmer and cook until you have roughly 1 cup (240 ml). Turn off the heat and allow to cool to room temperature.

Preheat your oven to 250°F (120°C). Line two 13 by 18-inch (33 by 46-cm) rimmed baking sheets with parchment paper.

Turn the ground pork out onto a large cutting board. Using a cleaver or chef's knife, chop the pork to loosen it up. Sprinkle the salt, pepper, and thyme over the pork, then chop it again. Scrape the pork off the board and into a mixing bowl. Add the mushroom mixture and mix thoroughly.

Divide the mixture evenly between the prepared baking sheets. Cover each pan loosely with plastic wrap and gently pat the mixture with your hands through the plastic wrap to spread it over the parchment. Using a small rolling pin, roll the mixture to an even thickness, roughly ⅛ to ¼ inch (3 to 6 mm). Remove and discard the plastic.

Place the baking sheets in the oven and bake for 1 hour, rotating the pans front to back halfway through. Remove the pans from the oven and slide the parchment with the pork off the pans and onto wire racks to cool for a few minutes. As soon as the meat is cool enough to handle, flip it over on the parchment in one piece. Slide the parchment back with the pork onto the baking sheets and return to the oven to bake for an additional 30 minutes. Remove from the oven and let cool to room temperature on the baking sheets.

When the meat has cooled to room temperature, slide the parchment with the pork onto a cutting board. Using a chef's knife or a pizza cutter, cut the meat into 2-inch (5-cm) squares.

Layer the squares in a covered container that allows a bit of airflow, separating the layers with parchment paper to keep the pieces from sticking together. Store in a cool, dark place for up to 2 weeks.

Bakkwa, also known as *rougan*, is a dried-meat specialty that originated in China but whose popularity has spread to Singapore, Malaysia, and other parts of Asia, where it is an immensely popular gift for the Lunar New Year celebration. There is a variety of *bakkwa* preparations, but we have grown quite fond of this chewy, savory-sweet ground pork version, glazed with honey and topped with sesame seeds.

Nearly as simple to prepare as any basic jerky, *bakkwa* is easily dried in a low oven. It may take a little practice to flatten the meat to an even thickness, but we find pieces that wind up a little too thick or too thin seem to disappear as quickly as the rest. *Bakkwa*, cut into squares, makes an attractive hors d'oeuvre. In addition to luck and prosperity in the New Year, you may find it also brings you the joy of new friends when served at your next cocktail party.

THE YEAR OF THE PIG

MAKES ABOUT 1½ POUNDS (680 G)

2 pounds (910 g) finely ground lean pork

1 teaspoon fine sea salt

2 teaspoons five-spice powder

¼ cup (60 ml) soy sauce

2 tablespoons fish sauce

1 tablespoon Shaoxing wine or dry sherry

½ teaspoon toasted sesame oil

6 tablespoons (125 g) honey

¼ cup (40 g) sesame seeds, lightly toasted

Preheat your oven to 250°F (120°C). Line two 13 by 18-inch (33 by 46-cm) rimmed baking sheets with parchment paper.

Turn the ground pork out onto a large cutting board. Using a cleaver or chef's knife, chop the pork to loosen it up. Sprinkle the pork with the salt, then chop it again. Scrape the seasoned pork off the board and into a mixing bowl. Add the five-spice powder, soy sauce, fish sauce, wine, and sesame oil and mix thoroughly.

Divide the mixture evenly between the prepared baking sheets. Cover each pan loosely with plastic wrap and gently pat the mixture with your hands through the plastic wrap to spread it over the parchment. Using a small rolling pin, roll the mixture to an even thickness, roughly ⅛ to ¼ inch (3 to 6 mm). Remove and discard the plastic.

In a small saucepan, warm the honey over low heat until it pours easily. Using a pastry brush, brush the surface of the pork with the honey. Sprinkle the sesame seeds evenly over the pork.

CONTINUED

Place the baking sheets in the oven and bake for 1 hour, rotating the pans front to back halfway through. Remove the pans from the oven and slide the parchment with the pork off the pans and onto wire racks to cool for a few minutes. As soon as the meat is cool enough to handle, flip it over on the parchment in one piece. Slide the parchment with the pork back onto the baking sheets and return to the oven to bake for an additional 30 minutes. Remove from the oven and let cool to room temperature on the baking sheets.

Slide the parchment with the pork onto a cutting board. Using a chef's knife or a pizza cutter, cut the meat into 2-inch (5-cm) squares.

Layer any *bakkwa* that isn't immediately devoured in a covered container that allows a bit of airflow, separating the layers with parchment paper to keep the pieces from sticking together. Store in a cool, dark place for up to 2 weeks.

YEAR OF THE PIG SANDWICH

Irresistible *bakkwa* never lasts long at our house, perhaps because for us it is an unusual treat. But apparently it is such a commonly exchanged Lunar New Year's gift that folks often wind up with more than they know what to do with. This phenomenon has sparked a series of articles on the Internet on what to do with your glut of CNY (short for Chinese New Year) jerky. People creatively repurpose this gift into inventive dishes, from fried rice to *banh mi*–style sandwiches (pictured at right).

This quirky jerky was inspired by a pot of Filipino-style duck adobo stew made over a campfire by our good friend chef Douglas Monsalud. We loved the tanginess of the vinegar with the rich, earthy flavor of the gizzards and wondered if we could translate those flavors into jerky. After a little trial and error, we struck upon this combination, dusted with black pepper, that keeps you reaching for another piece. We like to serve it as part of a mix of dried-meat specialties, along with some spicy roasted nuts and cold, crisp beer.

DUCK GIZZARD ADOBO

MAKES ABOUT 6 OUNCES (170 G)

12 ounces (340 g) duck gizzards

1 tablespoon fine sea salt

½ cup (120 ml) soy sauce

¼ cup (60 ml) water

¼ cup (60 ml) plantain or apple cider vinegar

5 cloves garlic, crushed

1 bay leaf

1 teaspoon black peppercorns, plus 2 teaspoons freshly ground black pepper

1 dried árbol or cayenne chile

Using a sharp paring knife, trim the gizzards of fat and silverskin (the thin, pearlescent membrane that covers the meat).

In a saucepan over medium heat, combine the gizzards, salt, soy sauce, water, vinegar, garlic, bay, the 1 teaspoon peppercorns, and the chile. Bring to a simmer, skimming off any foam that rises to the surface, then partially cover and cook, adjusting the heat as needed to maintain a simmer, until the gizzards are tender but not falling apart, about 1 hour. Remove from the heat and allow the gizzards to cool to room temperature in the liquid. Transfer the gizzards and liquid to a container, cover, and refrigerate overnight.

Drain the gizzards and discard the cooking liquid. Slice the gizzards into coins ¼ inch (6 mm) thick, then toss with the 2 teaspoons ground pepper.

Lay the gizzard slices on the racks of your dehydrator, making sure no slices are overlapping. Set the temperature to 145°F (63°C). Insert the racks into the dehydrator, leaving as much space as possible between them. Dehydrate for 1 hour, until the slices are firm but still chewy, rotating the racks front to back halfway through to ensure even drying.

Porchetta, the beloved Italian pork roast laden with garlic and herbs, is always a huge hit for dinner parties and special occasions. But its outer coating of crispy pork skin, known as *cotiche croccanti* in Italian, always seems to disappear from the serving platter faster than the meat. In a give-the-people-what-they-want move, we've devised this way of preparing just the pork skin *alla porchetta*. Serve the warm cracklins alongside an *aperitivo* or as part of an antipasto, or try crumbling them slightly and using to top cannellini beans or a simple green salad.

If you purchase whole skin-on pork legs to make jerky, you can save the leftover skin to make this recipe. Pork skin can also be purchased from most butcher shops. As it cooks in the oven, the skin gives off a fair amount of fat. Be sure to strain and refrigerate this fat to use for sautéing and frying.

PORCHETTA CRACKLINS

MAKES 8 TO 10 OUNCES (225 TO 280 G)

1 pound (450 g) pork skin with roughly ¼ inch (6 mm) of fat

3 cloves garlic

1 teaspoon fine sea salt

1 tablespoon chopped fresh rosemary

2 teaspoons fennel seed, toasted and ground

1 teaspoon finely ground black pepper

1 teaspoon flaky or coarse sea salt (such as Maldon or fleur de sel)

Grated zest of 2 lemons

Using a pair of sharp kitchen shears, cut the pork skin into strips 1 inch (2.5 cm) wide. Fit a rimmed baking sheet with a wire rack.

Bring a large pot of water to a boil. Add the pork skin and boil for 15 minutes. Using a slotted spoon, transfer the strips to the prepared wire rack, evenly spacing the pieces and making sure they are not overlapping. Refrigerate uncovered until dry, at least 4 hours or up to overnight.

Preheat your oven to 375°F (190°C).

Remove the pork skin from the refrigerator and place in a roasting pan. Place the pan in the oven and cook for about 1 hour, until the pork skin is golden brown. Reduce the oven temperature to 325°F (165°C) and cook until the skin is very crisp, about 45 minutes longer.

Meanwhile, using a mortar and pestle, pound the garlic with the fine salt to form a paste.

Remove the pan from the oven and add the garlic paste. Using a wooden spoon, stir until the pork skin is evenly coated. Return the pan to the oven and cook for 5 minutes longer.

Using tongs, carefully transfer the hot pork skin to a large bowl. Immediately add the rosemary, fennel seed, pepper, flaky or coarse salt, and lemon zest. Toss to coat.

These strips are best served hot and eaten right away, but they can be stored for up to 1 week. Allow to cool to room temperature, then transfer to a covered container that allows a bit of airflow and store in a cool, dark place. If you wish to reheat them for serving, arrange on a baking sheet and place in a 325°F (165°C) oven for about 10 minutes.

Many years ago, our good friend and stellar cook Isla Ruffo returned from a visit to her hometown in Sonora, Mexico, with a gift for us. It was a greasy plastic bag filled with what looked like wads of brown dog hair. "It's *machaca*, a traditional meat specialty," she said. I'm somewhat ashamed to say, but I think the bag was shoved into the back of a cabinet where it sat for several months. Then one stormy day, when there was little else in the house to cook, I finally considered what to do with it. Hunger is a great motivator, and within minutes, I was stuffing the rehydrated *machaca* into little burritos. The next day, we ate what was left with scrambled eggs. And just like that, we fell for *machaca*, big time. But *machaca* is not readily available stateside, so we set about making our own.

Machaca is derived from the Spanish word *machacar*, meaning "to pound" or "to crush". We won't lie; it takes quite a bit of pounding to turn leathery dried meat into the angelic fluffiness of *machaca*. A food processor is, unfortunately, no substitute for the old-school methods of whacking the beef repeatedly with a coarse stone or pulverizing it in a large *molcajete* (mortar) with a pestle. That's because the blade of the processor tears the beef into tiny pieces instead of leaving the muscle fibers intact.

Meat + Salt + Sun made with brisket or Carne Seca works best for this preparation. Relatively speaking, the brisket shreds easily and breaks apart quickly (but still, not that quickly) when pounded. Try it in Machacado con Huevos (page 105).

MACHACA

**MAKES 6 OUNCES
(170 G)**

6 ounces (170 g) Meat + Salt + Sun (page 28) or Carne Seca (page 31)

Time and tenacity

Using your hands, break the dried beef into rough bite-size pieces. Place a small handful of the pieces in a *molcajete* or other large stone mortar; do not overfill the *molcajete*, as too much can slow the process. Pound the pieces with the pestle until they break apart into individual threads. You may want to use your hands to shred the pieces further. Remove the *machaca* from the *molcajete* and repeat with the remaining pieces of meat.

Use right away, or transfer to a covered container that allows a bit of airflow, preferably with a desiccant packet (see page 25), and store in a cool, dark place for up to 2 weeks. Alternatively, place the *machaca* in a zipper-lock bag, seal well, and freeze for up to 3 months.

This unique Chinese dried-meat specialty, sometimes called "pork floss" or *rousong*, is used to fill buns and sticky rice rolls, top tofu, and as a condiment for congee. Although you can find it sold by the tubful at some Asian grocery stores, these commercial versions tend to contain frightening amounts of preservatives, so we've tried our hand at making a homemade version with tasty results.

In this recipe, the meat is first braised to make it easier to shred finely, and then, unlike most other dried meats, it is dehydrated on the stove top in a wok or pan. The finished fluffy pork is a melt-in-your-mouth topping for Rice Porridge (page 94).

FLUFFY PORK

MAKES ABOUT 1 POUND (450 G)

2 pounds (910 g) pork sirloin, cut into 1½-inch (4-cm) cubes

1 teaspoon fine sea salt

2 cups (480 ml) chicken broth

2 tablespoons soy sauce

2 tablespoons dark soy sauce

1 tablespoon honey

1 tablespoon Shaoxing wine or sherry

4 green onions, cut into 2-inch (5-cm) lengths

1-inch (2.5-cm) piece peeled fresh ginger

2 whole star anise

1 teaspoon Szechuan peppercorns

1 teaspoon coriander seed

Season the pork with the salt. Place the meat in a saucepan and add the chicken broth, soy sauce, dark soy sauce, honey, wine, green onions, ginger, and spices. Cover and bring to a simmer over medium heat. Lower the heat to medium-low and simmer gently until the pork is fork-tender, 1½ to 2 hours. Remove from the heat and allow the meat to cool to room temperature in its liquid.

Using a slotted spoon, transfer the meat to a gallon-size (3.8-L) plastic bag, leaving the braising liquid in the pan. Set the pan over low heat and simmer the liquid until reduced to roughly ¼ to ⅓ cup (60 to 75 ml). It should be thick and syrupy.

Lay the bag with the pork flat on a countertop. Using a rolling pin or a rubber mallet, pound the meat until it falls apart. Empty the pork into a bowl and further shred the meat by hand until it separates into individual strands or fibers. Pour the reduced braising liquid over the meat and mix by hand to coat evenly.

Heat a large cast-iron or nonstick skillet or well-seasoned wok over low heat. Transfer the meat to the pan and cook, stirring frequently, until dry, somewhat fluffy, and a shade or two darker in color, 30 to 40 minutes. Remove from the heat and allow to cool to room temperature in the pan.

Use right away, or transfer to a covered container that allows a bit of airflow, making sure not to pack the pork too tightly, and store in a cool, dark place for up to 1 week. Alternatively, place the pork in a zipper-lock bag, seal well, and freeze for up to 3 months.

Biltong is a dried game-meat specialty that originates in South Africa. Like many indigenous populations, the people of southern Africa preserved their meat by salting it and leaving it to air- or sun-dry. With the arrival of Dutch settlers in the late seventeenth century, the idea of brining or marinating meat in vinegar, sugar, and spices took hold. The acidity of vinegar and the antimicrobial properties of spices helped further preserve the meat in a climate where spoilage was a vexing problem.

To make traditional *biltong*, you will need access to wild game, such as antelope, deer, or elk. Today, however, most *biltong* is made with beef; you can certainly use beef bottom round in this recipe.

BILTONG

MAKES ABOUT 1 POUND (450 G)

1 tablespoon plus 1 teaspoon fine sea salt

2 teaspoons brown sugar

1 tablespoon coriander seed, toasted and lightly crushed

1 teaspoon freshly ground black pepper

2 tablespoons red wine vinegar

2 pounds (910 g) trimmed lean antelope, venison, or elk, cut into strips 1½ to 2 inches (4 to 5 cm) in diameter and 6 to 8 inches (15 to 20 cm) long

In a wide, shallow bowl, mix together the salt, sugar, coriander, pepper, and vinegar. Add the strips of meat and, using your hands, mix well to evenly coat the strips. Cover and refrigerate for at least 3 hours or up to overnight.

When you are ready to dry the meat, remove it from the refrigerator. Remove the strips from the marinade, letting the excess liquid drain off. Some of the coriander and black pepper should adhere to the meat. Place the strips on the racks of your dehydrator, making sure that no strips are overlapping or touching. Set the temperature to 145°F (63°C). Insert the racks into the dehydrator, leaving as much space as possible between them. Dehydrate for 3 to 4 hours, until the *biltong* is very firm, flipping the strips and rotating the racks front to back halfway through to ensure even drying.

Allow the *biltong* to cool at room temperature. To serve, cut the strips crosswise into thin slices; cut only as much as you plan to eat. Transfer any uncut *biltong* to a covered container that allows a bit of airflow and store in a cool, dark place for up to 6 weeks.

Tasajo is a traditional air-dried meat from western Spain's Extremadura region. It is typically made using strips of lean goat, beef, wild boar, or, as in this version, venison. Another specialty of the Extremadura region is *pimentón de la Vera*, the gorgeous red paprika made by grinding smoked and dried chiles from the La Vera valley. Unsurprisingly, *pimentón* is the predominant spice in this *tasajo*. In addition to imparting a wonderful smoky flavor, the paprika has antimicrobial properties and acts as a natural preservative. *Tasajo* is perfect served along with a sharp cheese and a bowl of olives at the start of a meal.

TASAJO CON PIMENTÓN

MAKES ABOUT 1 POUND (450 G)

1 tablespoon plus 1 teaspoon fine sea salt

2 tablespoons dried oregano, crumbled

2 pounds (910 g) trimmed lean venison leg, cut into strips 1½ to 2 inches (4 to 5 cm) in diameter and 6 to 8 inches (15 to 20 cm) long

2 tablespoons dry sherry

¼ cup (35 g) sweet (dulce) pimentón de la Vera

In a large, shallow bowl, combine the salt and oregano. Add the strips of meat, rolling them around in the seasonings to coat evenly. Add the sherry and, using your hands, mix well to evenly coat the meat. Cover and refrigerate overnight.

Place the *pimentón* in a baking dish. Remove the meat from the refrigerator and dredge each strip in the *pimentón* to evenly coat.

Cut 12-inch (30-cm) lengths of butcher's twine; you will need as many pieces as you have meat strips. Using a trussing needle or sharp metal skewer, pierce a hole in each strip about 1 inch (2.5 cm) from one end. Thread a length of butcher's twine through the hole, then tie the two ends together to form a loop.

Hang the meat strips by their twine loops in a cool, dark, ventilated location, preferably one with a stable temperature of 50°F to 60°F (10°C to 16°C); in the late autumn through the early spring, we've used our garage with excellent results. Allow to air-dry until the *tasajo* is firm but not too hard (roughly the texture of a salami), about 10 days. If the temperature is a little cooler, drying may take up to 2 weeks; if the temperature is slightly warmer, it may take only 1 week.

To serve, cut the strips crosswise into thin slices; cut only as much as you plan to eat. Wrap any uncut *tasajo* in plastic wrap and store in the refrigerator for up to 3 weeks.

These spiced duck breasts were one of the first whole-muscle dry-curing projects we tried, and we've been loving them ever since. Over the years, we've slightly adjusted the seasonings, but the process has remained more or less the same.

Duck breasts are perfectly sized for air-drying at home and a good cut to start with for anyone new to curing meat. They are relatively small and flat, which means they dry quickly and evenly. From start to finish, the process takes just a little over 2 weeks. For your minimal effort and small investment of time, you will be richly rewarded. Thinly sliced, the flavorful meat, with its layer of buttery fat, is a wonderful addition to a charcuterie board, salads, hors d'oeuvres, and sandwiches.

SPICED DUCK BREASTS

MAKES 2 DUCK BREASTS

1 teaspoon black peppercorns

1 teaspoon coriander seed

3 allspice berries

1 teaspoon yellow mustard seed

1 teaspoon juniper berries

1 tablespoon fine sea salt

½ teaspoon curing salt #2

½ teaspoon dried oregano

2 skin-on duck breasts, each about 12 ounces (340 g), with the tenders removed

2 cloves garlic, crushed

¼ cup (60 ml) red wine

In a skillet over low heat, toast the peppercorns, coriander, allspice, mustard, and juniper until fragrant. Allow to cool to room temperature. Using a spice grinder, pulverize the spices to a fine powder. In a large, shallow bowl, combine the ground spices with the sea salt, curing salt, and oregano.

Add the duck breasts to the spice mixture, turning them to evenly coat. Add the garlic and red wine. Cover and refrigerate for 3 days, turning the breasts each day to ensure even seasoning.

Remove the duck breasts from the refrigerator. Wrap each breast in a double layer of cheesecloth. Tie each end tightly with butcher's twine, leaving a loop at one end for hanging.

Hang the duck breasts in a cool, dark, ventilated location, preferably one with a stable temperature of 50°F to 60°F (10°C to 16°C); in the late autumn though the early spring, we've used our garage with excellent results. Allow to air-dry until the breasts are firm like salami, about 2 weeks. If the temperature is a little cooler, drying may take up to 1 week longer; if the temperature is slightly warmer, it may take only 10 days.

To serve, unwrap the duck breasts and cut crosswise into thin slices; cut only as much as you plan to eat. Wrap any uncut portions in plastic wrap and store in the refrigerator for up to 3 weeks.

Brési is traditional air-dried beef from the mountainous Jura region that straddles France and Switzerland. A cousin of Italian *bresaola* and German *Bündnerfleisch*, *brési* is customarily cold smoked in between its initial salt curing and the finishing stages of air-drying. The wood smoke perfumes the meat, but it also aids in its preservation because it slows the growth of harmful organisms and creates a protective layer that prevents the growth of unwanted mold and bacteria.

The finished *brési* has a deep burgundy center and an earthy, delicately smoky flavor. It is typically sliced very thinly and eaten alongside locally produced Gruyère cheese or as an accompaniment to fondue. We also love this air-dried beef in salads, such as Arugula Salad with Fuyu Persimmon and Brési (page 106), or cooked with creamy béchamel sauce and wild mushrooms for Creamed Chipped Beef on Toast (page 102).

BRÉSI

MAKES 1 EYE OF ROUND

1 whole beef eye of round, trimmed of all exterior fat and silverskin

1 tablespoon dried thyme

1 tablespoon black peppercorns

2 bay leaves, crumbled

2 tablespoons plus 2 teaspoons fine sea salt

1 teaspoon curing salt #2

Remove the beef from the refrigerator. Using a sharp metal skewer, pierce the surface of the beef on all sides to a depth of about ½ inch (12 mm), covering it completely with perforations spaced about ½ inch (12 mm) apart. Let the beef stand at room temperature for about 45 minutes. This will allow the muscle fibers to relax and will make it easier for the seasonings to penetrate.

Meanwhile, using a spice grinder, pulverize the thyme, peppercorns, and bay to a fine powder. In a dish large enough to accommodate the beef, stir together the ground spices, the sea salt, and the curing salt.

Lay the beef in the dish and turn to coat with the seasonings. Massage the seasonings into the beef, then let stand at room temperature for an additional 30 minutes. Transfer the beef and any excess seasoning to a large zipper-lock bag, seal well, and refrigerate for 2 weeks. Each day, open the bag and rotate the meat to ensure even seasoning and curing.

After 2 weeks, remove the beef from the bag, discarding any excess seasoning. Wrap the meat in a double layer of cheesecloth. Tie each end tightly with butcher's twine, leaving a loop at one end for hanging. Cold smoke the beef by hanging it in a smoker or over the embers of a fire; allow to cold smoke for about 3 hours. Periodically check the internal temperature of the beef by inserting a meat thermometer into the center; the internal temperature should not exceed 60°F (16°C). If the beef starts to get too warm, take it away from the smoke and cool down the fire down by adding a little water or by simply allowing it to die down. It's better to smoke the beef for less time than to allow it to start to cook, so err on the side of less smoke.

Once done smoking, hang the beef in a cool, dark, ventilated location, preferably one with a temperature of 50°F to 60°F (10°C to 16°C); in the late autumn through early spring, we've used our garage with excellent results. Allow to air-dry until the meat is firm but not rock hard, 4 to 6 weeks. If the temperature is a little cooler, drying may take a little longer; if the temperature is slightly warmer, it may go more quickly.

To serve, unwrap the beef. Using a meat slicer, mandoline, or sharp knife, slice the meat crosswise as thinly as possible; cut only as much as you plant to eat. *Brési* is best when freshly sliced, as the slices tend to oxidize and dry out quickly. Wrap the uncut portion in plastic wrap and refrigerate for up to 2 months.

CHAPTER FOUR

COOKING WITH JERKY

Rice porridge, or congee, is a common breakfast food in many parts of East and Southeast Asia. This silky, savory bowl of comfort with its spicy, salty, crunchy toppings beats the pants off the oatmeal we had to plod through at the breakfast table as kids. Toppings for rice porridge may vary from pickled mustard greens and preserved eggs to fried shallots and dried shrimp, but pork floss is always a favorite.

RICE PORRIDGE WITH FLUFFY PORK

SERVES 4

Porridge

10 cups (2.4 L) chicken or pork broth

1¾ cups (340 g) jasmine rice

1 tablespoon fish sauce, plus more if needed

Fine sea salt

Toppings

1⅓ cups (150 g) Fluffy Pork (page 84)

2 green onions, thinly sliced on the diagonal

2 tablespoons peeled and julienned fresh ginger

1 or 2 red Thai chiles, chopped

½ cup (70 g) chopped roasted peanuts

Small handful fresh cilantro sprigs

To make the porridge, in a large saucepan over medium heat, bring the broth to a boil. Add the rice and stir until the broth returns to a simmer. Add the fish sauce, turn down the heat to low, and cook uncovered, stirring frequently, until the rice is very tender and beginning to break apart, 25 to 30 minutes. The porridge should pour easily from a spoon; if it's too thick, adjust the consistency with hot water. Taste for seasoning and add salt or more fish sauce, if desired.

To serve, arrange the toppings on a platter and set on the table. Ladle the porridge into warmed serving bowls and let everyone garnish his or her own bowl at the table.

In Oaxaca, lightly dried *cecina adobada* is often served along with another traditional Oaxacan specialty, *enfrijoladas*, a variation on enchiladas made by dipping corn tortillas in pureed black beans. For a traditional Mexican brunch, serve the *enfrijoladas* with mugs of steaming spiced hot chocolate or *café de olla* (spiced, sweetened coffee).

ENFRIJOLADAS CON CECINA

SERVES 4

Enfrijoladas

1¼ cups (255 g) dried black beans

Fine sea salt

5 cloves garlic, unpeeled

4 tablespoons (55 g) lard or bacon fat

1 white onion, halved and thinly sliced

1 small árbol or cayenne chile

1 small sprig epazote (optional)

12 corn tortillas

Cecina and Toppings

12 ounces (340 g) lightly dried Cecina Adobada (page 62)

¼ cup (55 g) crème fraîche

1 cup (150 g) crumbled queso fresco or Cotija cheese

¼ cup (5 g) fresh cilantro leaves

1 small white onion, sliced into thin rings, or pickled red onion (optional)

To make the *enfrijoladas*, rinse the beans well, then drain. Put the beans in a large bowl, add water to cover by about 2 inches (5 cm), and allow to soak at room temperature for at least 4 hours or up to overnight.

Pour off the soaking water, place the beans in a pot, and add water to cover by about 2 inches (5 cm). Bring to a simmer over medium heat. Lower the heat slightly to maintain a slow simmer and cook uncovered. Monitor the progress of the beans every 30 minutes for the first hour and every 15 minutes after that. Different beans cook at different rates. When the beans are slightly softened but not fully tender, season to taste with salt and continue to simmer until the beans have tender skins and creamy interiors. Remove from the heat and set aside.

In a dry skillet over low heat, toast the garlic cloves, occasionally shaking the pan, until the skins are spotted brown and the garlic is soft. Allow to cool, then peel. In the same skillet, melt 1 tablespoon of the lard over medium heat. Add the onion, árbol chile, and epazote, season lightly with salt, and cook, stirring occasionally, until the onion has softened, about 10 minutes. Transfer the onion mixture to a blender and add the peeled garlic cloves and the black beans, and their cooking liquid. Puree until smooth.

In a sauté pan or large, wide saucepan over low heat, melt 1 tablespoon of the lard. Pour the pureed beans into the pan and heat, stirring frequently. The warm puree should be thick but pour easily from a ladle. If it seems too thick, add a little hot water to thin. If it seems too thin, cook, stirring frequently, until the mixture reduces and thickens. Taste for seasoning and add salt, if needed.

CONTINUED

In a skillet over medium heat, melt the remaining 2 tablespoons lard. Add a tortilla and fry for about 10 seconds on each side to soften, then carefully transfer to a plate. Repeat with the remaining tortillas, stacking them on the plate as they are done.

Preheat your oven to its lowest setting and place four oven-safe plates on the racks to warm.

Using tongs and working with one at a time, dip the tortillas into the bean puree to coat on both sides, then transfer to the heated plates, placing 3 tortillas on each. Return the plates to the oven to keep the *enfrijoladas* warm while you cook the *cecina*.

To prepare the *cecina*, heat a large cast-iron skillet over high heat. Sear the *cecina* just until heated through, 20 to 30 seconds per side.

Remove the plates of *enfrijoladas* from the oven. Arrange the *cecina* on the *enfrijoladas*, dividing it evenly. Top with the crème fraîche, crumbled cheese, cilantro, and onion. Serve immediately.

SEASONING WHEN COOKING WITH JERKY

Jerky and other dried meats tend to be highly seasoned, so when using them as an ingredient, you need to take into account their saltiness. Use a light hand when adding salt and pepper and taste often while cooking.

This rich, soulful stew of meat and beans is considered the national dish of Brazil, where it is often eaten as part of a celebratory meal. Variations abound and the ingredients range from pig's tails to blood sausages to bananas. But most Brazilians would agree that sun-dried beef, known as *carne de sol*, is an integral component. It truly adds depth of flavor as well as a unique texture that makes the dish extraordinarily satisfying.

A pot of *feijoada* is perfect for feeding a large crowd, especially when served with simple traditional accompaniments, such as rice, braised greens, slices of pineapple, orange wedges, and pickled chiles.

FEIJOADA

SERVES 8 TO 10

2 pounds (910 g) oxtails

1 pound (450 g) pork stew meat

Fine sea salt

2¼ cups (450 g) dried black beans

1 large smoked ham hock

1 bay leaf

2 tablespoons lard or bacon fat

1 large yellow onion, diced

3 or 4 cloves garlic, finely chopped

2 medium red bell peppers, seeded and diced

6 to 8 ounces (170 to 225 g) Meat + Salt + Sun (page 28) or other simply seasoned beef jerky, torn into bite-size pieces

4 cups (960 ml) beef broth or water

1 unpeeled orange, quartered

8 to 10 ounces linguiça or cured chorizo, cut into coins

The day before you plan to cook the stew, rub the oxtails and pork stew meat liberally with salt. Place in a wide, shallow bowl, cover, and refrigerate. Rinse the beans well, then drain. Put the beans in a large bowl, add water to cover by about 2 inches (5 cm), and allow to soak at room temperature.

The following day, drain the beans and place in a large pot. Add the ham hock and bay leaf, then add water to cover by about 2 inches (5 cm). Bring to a simmer over medium heat, skimming off any foam that rises to the surface. Lower the heat to maintain a gentle simmer and cook, uncovered, until the beans are tender and the meat of the ham hock begins to pull away from the bone, 1½ to 2 hours. Season to taste with salt. Allow the beans to cool slightly, then remove the hock. Shred the meat off of the bone, then return the meat to the pot; discard the bone.

While the beans and ham hock simmer, remove the oxtails and pork stew meat from the refrigerator and bring to room temperature. In a large, deep pot or Dutch oven over medium heat, melt the lard. Working in batches and being careful not to crowd the pot, add the oxtails and stew meat and brown on all sides, about 10 minutes per batch. As the pieces are ready, transfer them to a large plate.

CONTINUED

After all of the meat has been browned, add the onion and garlic to the pot along with a pinch of salt. Cook, stirring with a wooden spoon and scraping up any browned meaty bits on the bottom of the pot, until the onion is golden, about 10 minutes. Add the bell peppers and continue cooking, stirring occasionally, until the onion and peppers have softened, about 5 minutes. Add the dried beef and return the oxtails and stew meat to the pot. Add the orange and broth and bring to a simmer. Lower the heat to maintain a gentle simmer, cover, and continue to cook until the meat is nearly tender, about 2 hours. Add the linguiça and the ham hock meat and beans with their cooking liquid and continue to simmer for another 30 minutes, until all of the meat is quite tender. Taste for seasoning and add more salt, if needed. Ladle the *feijoada* into bowls and serve.

MORE WAYS TO COOK WITH JERKY

The recipes in this chapter are just a few of our favorite ways to cook with jerky and other dried meats. But there are many ways to incorporate jerky into your everyday cooking.

- Try shredding a jerky, such as Bourbon and Molasses Smoked Beef Jerky (page 38), and adding to your favorite recipe for baked beans

- Chop up Pocket Pastrami (page 61) or Cecina Adobada (page 62) and fry with peppers, onions, and potatoes for a breakfast hash

- Shred Pork Teriyaki (page 37) or Pork with Fermented Chile and Miso Sauce (page 64) and add to fried rice

- Make a green papaya salad using shredded Lemongrass Beef (page 53) or Dendeng Balado (page 54)

- Add diced Prairie Bison (page 36) or Pork Pique-nique (page 41) to enrich a tomato sauce

- Prepare a traditional Cuban *tasajo criollo*, using shredded Meat + Salt + Sun (page 28) or Carne Seca (page 31) cooked with peppers, onions, tomato, and a splash of sour orange juice; serve with plantains and rice or use as a filling for empanadas

Notorious for being slopped out in military chow halls and mess decks of yesteryear, creamed chipped beef on toast (aka sh*t on a shingle) gets a bad rap. But if prepared using commercially processed "chipped" or sliced beef and other unsavory ingredients, perhaps the rap is deserved. However, if you use delicate slices of *brési* and dried wild mushrooms and spoon it over slices of good bread, your chipped beef will be working on a whole other level. This is an excellent breakfast dish that's equally good as a light lunch or dinner, with a green salad served alongside. You can spoon the creamed chipped beef over baked potatoes instead of bread, if you wish.

The dried beef is best sliced on a meat slicer, but you can get reasonably thin slices using a mandoline.

CREAMED CHIPPED BEEF ON TOAST

SERVES 4

1 ounce (30 g) dried wild mushrooms

3 tablespoons unsalted butter

1½ cups (285 g) minced yellow onion

Fine sea salt

2 tablespoons all-purpose flour

1 tablespoon dry sherry

2 cups (480 ml) whole milk

3 ounces (85 g) Brési (page 90) or other air-dried beef, very thinly sliced and cut into ribbons ½ inch (12 mm) wide

1 tablespoon chopped fresh thyme

4 large slices pain au levain or other hearty rustic bread, toasted

2 tablespoons chopped fresh parsley

Freshly ground black pepper

Put the mushrooms in a small bowl, add cold water to cover them by about 1 inch (2.5 cm), and let rehydrate at room temperature for at least 3 hours or up to overnight. Using your hands or a slotted spoon, gently remove the mushrooms from their soaking liquid, leaving any grit in the bottom of the bowl. Strain the soaking liquid through a fine-mesh sieve and set aside. Pat the mushrooms dry and chop finely.

Preheat your oven to its lowest setting and place four oven-safe plates on the racks to warm.

In a saucepan over low heat, melt the butter. Add the onion and cook, stirring occasionally, until softened and translucent, about 10 minutes. Season with a pinch of salt, then sift the flour into the pan and stir to combine with the onion. While whisking constantly, gradually add the sherry, followed by the milk. Bring to a simmer and continue to whisk until the mixture is smooth and thick enough to coat the back of a wooden spoon, 8 to 10 minutes. Fold in the beef, thyme, and the chopped mushrooms and cook until the beef has softened, about 10 minutes longer. Taste for seasoning and add more salt, if needed.

Remove the plates from the oven and place a slice of toast on each. Divide the chipped beef evenly among the plates, spooning it over the toast. Garnish with the parsley and freshly ground black pepper. Serve immediately.

There are many delicious *machaca* preparations, but this simple, classic Sonoran-style fry-up of onions, roasted poblano chiles, tomatoes, and dried beef topped with an egg might be our favorite. It's a hearty breakfast, fit for a vaquero who's heading out to round up cattle in the high desert country or ample enough to fuel you for a morning of making more jerky.

MACHACADO CON HUEVOS

SERVES 4

3 tablespoons lard, bacon fat, or suet

1 white onion, diced

5 cloves garlic, chopped

Fine sea salt

3 poblano chiles, roasted, peeled, seeded, and diced

4 plum tomatoes, cored and diced

6 ounces (170 g) Machaca (page 82)

4 large eggs

Flour tortillas, warmed, for serving

To make the *machacado*, in a sauté pan over medium heat, warm 2 tablespoons of the lard. Add the onion and garlic, season lightly with salt, and cook, stirring occasionally, until the onion has softened, about 10 minutes. Add the roasted chiles and tomatoes and cook, stirring occasionally, until the tomatoes have softened and released their liquid, about 5 minutes. Fold in the *machaca* and cook until the *machaca* is tender and has sopped up all of the moisture, 5 to 10 minutes. Taste for seasoning and add more salt, if needed. Remove from the heat, cover to keep warm, and set aside while you fry the eggs.

To fry the eggs, in a well-seasoned cast-iron skillet over medium heat, warm the remaining 1 tablespoon lard. Crack the eggs, one at a time, into different areas of the skillet and fry until done to your liking. Season each egg with a pinch of salt.

Divide the *machacado* among four plates or shallow bowls and top each serving with a fried egg. Serve immediately with flour tortillas.

MACHACADO WITH SCRAMBLED EGGS

Crack 8 large eggs into a bowl and whisk together with a splash of heavy cream and a pinch of salt. Using a large skillet, prepare the *machacado* following the recipe above. When the *machaca* is tender, add the beaten eggs to the pan and gently stir until the eggs form soft curds, about 5 minutes. Divide the mixture among four plates or shallow bowls and serve with warm tortillas.

For a few weeks in the late autumn, you can't throw a stone in our neighborhood without hitting a ripe persimmon. They hang from the nearly naked trees in bright orange defiance of the cold winds and first storms of the season. Friends gift them by the shopping bagful, along with jars of homemade persimmon butter. Even our weekly farm-share box brims with the glowing, sweet fruit.

The squat, tomato-shaped Fuyu persimmon is prized for salads because, unlike many other varieties of persimmon, it remains somewhat crisp and firm when ripe. An autumn favorite, this elegant composed salad pairs earthy air-dried beef with the bright, sweet flavor of the Fuyu. You can also prepare this salad with thin slivers of Spiced Duck Breasts (page 88) in place of the beef.

ARUGULA SALAD WITH FUYU PERSIMMON AND BRÉSI

SERVES 4 TO 6

2 or 3 ripe Fuyu persimmons, peeled and sliced into thin rounds

4 tablespoons (60 ml) olive oil, plus more for drizzling

2 tablespoons aged balsamic vinegar, plus more for drizzling

Flaky or coarse sea salt (such as Maldon or fleur de sel)

4 ounces (115 g) Brési (page 90), bresaola, or other air-dried beef, thinly sliced

4 cups (85 g) arugula, washed and dried

Freshly ground black pepper

2 ounces (55 g) Parmigiano-Reggiano cheese, in shards

Arrange the persimmon slices on a large platter. Drizzle with a bit of the olive oil and balsamic vinegar and season with a pinch of salt. Lay the slices of *brési* on top of the persimmons.

In a bowl, toss the arugula with the 4 tablespoons (60 ml) olive oil and the 2 tablespoons balsamic vinegar and season to taste with salt and pepper. Place the dressed arugula on the bed of persimmons and *brési* and scatter the cheese about the platter. Drizzle with olive oil and dot with additional drops of balsamic and serve immediately, or serve the salad with additional olive oil and balsamic on the side so everyone may dress to his or her liking.

We have been making some version of this gingery peanut-laced cabbage slaw for many years. Easy to prepare with ingredients we often have on hand, it makes a frequent appearance at our dinner table alongside grilled meats, noodles, or rice. Originally, we used salted dried shrimp to flavor this salad, but smoky, peppery *ganba* is a surprisingly suitable substitution and makes this salad almost a meal in itself.

GINGERY CABBAGE SLAW WITH SMOKY BEEF AND HERBS

SERVES 4

4 ounces (115 g) Ganba (page 50) or other dried beef, torn into bite-size pieces

¼ cup (25 g) peeled and julienned fresh ginger

2 green onions, julienned

1 or 2 red or green Thai chiles, minced

1 large carrot, peeled and julienned

6 cups (700 g) shredded napa cabbage

1 tablespoon fish sauce

Juice of 2 limes

1 teaspoon honey

¼ cup (5 g) chopped fresh cilantro

2 tablespoons chopped fresh mint

¼ cup (35 g) chopped toasted peanuts

Fine sea salt

Using a mortar and pestle, pound the dried beef until it splinters and shreds. Alternatively, place the dried beef in the workbowl of a food processor and pulse until finely shredded.

In a large bowl, combine the shredded beef, the ginger, green onions, chile(s), carrot, and cabbage. In a small bowl, stir together the fish sauce, lime juice, and honey and pour over the cabbage mixture. Using your hands, toss the slaw to distribute the dressing. Let sit for 10 to 15 minutes to allow the vegetables to soften slightly and absorb the dressing.

Fold the cilantro, mint, and peanuts into the slaw. Taste for seasoning and add more salt, if needed. Serve immediately.

For the past twenty years, we've been using fragrant *injera* bread to scoop up delicious *meser wot* and other Ethiopian specialties at Café Colucci in Oakland, California. It was there that we first encountered *quanta*, which the café cooks simmer in a buttery *berbere*-spiced sauce, and realized that dried meats could be used as an ingredient in cooking. *Meser wot*, sometimes spelled *misir wot*, is a thick, spice-laden lentil stew that is commonly prepared as a vegetarian dish. We were intrigued when we came across a meaty version made with *quanta* and were easily won over by its rich, vibrant flavors. For a traditional Ethiopian feast, serve a salad and one or two other vegetables alongside, and plenty of *injera*. Or for a simpler meal, serve the *meser wot* over rice or another hearty grain.

QUANTA MESER WOT

SERVES 4 TO 6

1 cup (190 g) red lentils
(aka pink lentils or masoor dal)

½ teaspoon ground turmeric

5 cups (1.2 L) water

Seeds of 2 cardamom pods

1 whole clove

1-inch (2.5-cm) piece
cinnamon stick

1 teaspoon fenugreek seed

3 or 4 dried bird's-eye or
cayenne chiles

1 tablespoon unsalted butter

1 large yellow onion, diced

3 cloves garlic, finely chopped

Fine sea salt

6 to 8 ounces (170 to 225 g)
Quanta (page 67), shredded
into bite-size pieces

6 plum tomatoes, diced

In a saucepan, combine the lentils, turmeric, and water. Bring to a simmer over medium heat and cook, stirring occasionally and skimming any foam that may rise to the surface, until the lentils are soft enough to mash with the back of a spoon, about 30 minutes. Cover and set aside.

While the lentils are simmering, in a dry skillet over low heat, toast the cardamom, clove, cinnamon, fenugreek, and chiles until fragrant. Allow to cool to room temperature. Using a spice grinder, pulverize the spices until finely ground.

In a large sauté pan over medium heat, melt the butter. Add the onion and garlic, season lightly with salt, and cook, stirring occasionally, until the onion has softened, about 10 minutes. Add the *quanta* and the ground spices and cook, stirring occasionally, until the meat begins to soften, about 5 minutes. Add the tomatoes and continue cooking for an additional 10 minutes. Stir in the lentils and their cooking liquid and bring to a simmer. Turn down the heat to low and cook, stirring occasionally, until the lentils have thickened and the *quanta* has softened, 15 to 20 minutes. Taste for seasoning and add more salt, if needed. Serve immediately.

Pemmican was the clever invention of native North Americans. Traditionally, bits of lean dried meat were pounded with fruit or other nutritious foods and then combined with animal fats to create a protein-packed, nutrient-dense meal on the go. In this modern adaptation, creamy coconut oil replaces the more traditional rendered animal fat, and honey provides a touch of sweetness. The result is a delicious energy bar that you can tote along for a quick boost.

PECAN-DATE PEMMICAN

MAKES ABOUT 1½ POUNDS (680 G)

¾ cup (220 g) coconut oil

¼ cup (85 g) honey

8 ounces (225 g) bison or beef jerky, such as Prairie Bison (page 36) or Meat + Salt + Sun (page 28), torn into bite-size pieces

1 cup (110 g) chopped toasted pecans

1 cup (150 g) pitted and diced dates

¼ cup (40 g) sesame seeds

In a small saucepan over low heat, warm the coconut oil and honey until liquefied. Remove from the heat and set aside.

Place the jerky in the workbowl of a food processor and process until very finely chopped. Add the pecans, dates, and sesame seeds and pulse a few times to combine. Continue pulsing while slowly pouring the coconut oil–honey mixture through the feed tube, then process until the mixture begins to hold together, about 1 minute.

Line a 13 by 18-inch (33 by 46-cm) rimmed baking sheet with wax or parchment paper. Transfer the mixture to the pan and, using your hands, gently press it into an even thickness, about ½ inch (12 mm).

Alternatively, using your hands, roll the mixture into 1-inch (2.5-cm) balls and place on the prepared baking sheet.

Refrigerate the pemmican until firm, about 1 hour. If you pressed the mixture into a baking sheet, use a chef's knife to cut it into triangles or rectangles.

Place the pemmican in an airtight container and store in a cool, dark place for up to 3 weeks, or in the refrigerator for up to 2 months.

RESOURCES

MEATS

Broken Arrow Ranch
brokenarrowranch.com
(800) 962-4263

Fatted Calf Charcuterie
fattedcalf.com
Napa, CA
(707) 256-3684

San Francisco, CA
(415) 400-5614

Heritage Foods USA
heritagefoodsusa.com
(718) 389-0985

NorthStar Bison
northstarbison.com
(888) 295-6332

Paradise Locker Meats
paradisemeats.com
(816) 370-MEAT

SEASONINGS AND SPECIALTY INGREDIENTS

Rancho Gordo New World Specialty Food
ranchogordo.com
(800) 599-8323

Whole Spice
wholespice.com
(707) 778-1750

Wine Forest Wild Foods
wineforest.com
(707) 944-8604

JERKY MAKING EQUIPMENT AND SUPPLIES

Butcher & Packer
butcher-packer.com
(248) 583-1250

The Sausage Maker
sausagemaker.com
(888) 490-8525

ACKNOWLEDGMENTS

We feel pretty lucky that occasionally our "workday" consists of spending time with each other, dreaming up delicious meaty goods, cooking at home with the stereo blasting, and sitting by the fire, watching the magic of jerky happen.

One could not have asked for a more supportive crew than Team Jerky, led by our most enthusiastic editor, Emily Timberlake, with technical support from Anne Goldberg and the keen eye of Angelina Cheney. Their work, along with the occasional wise anecdote from Aaron Wehner, and the helpful prodding of our agent Katherine Cowles, kept the wheels on the cart.

As much as we adore jerky, we will be the first to admit that it isn't the most photogenic subject matter. Yet, Ed Anderson managed to capture its most mouthwatering, primal essence in his gorgeous photographs.

There is an extraordinary network of farmers, ranchers, and processors that work unbelievably hard to help us bring good food to the table. We could not have made this book without the people from Heritage Foods U.S.A., Five Dot Ranch, Richards Grassfed, Paradise Locker Meats, McCormack Ranch, Riverdog Farm, Broken Arrow Ranch, Liberty Duck, Mariquita Farm, and more.

We are incredibly grateful to our Fatted Calf family. Ren Rossini loaned us her mom's old dehydrator when ours unexpectedly retired, Peter Chenaux and Lody Gonzalez dealt with all of our oddball meat requests, Bailie kept the house in order, and everyone provided invaluable feedback and made sure no jerky went to waste while we were recipe testing this book.

Sean Smith, our dear friend, we miss you terribly. We promise to keep Sho Sho, Scarlet, and Magenta well fed.

Promote peace, preach love, and make jerky forever!

INDEX

Published in the United States by Ten Speed Press, an imprint of the
Crown Publishing Group, a division of Penguin Random House LLC, New York.
www.crownpublishing.com
www.tenspeed.com

Ten Speed Press and the Ten Speed Press colophon are registered
trademarks of Penguin Random House LLC.

Library of Congress Cataloging-in-Publication Data is on file with
the publisher.

Hardcover ISBN: 978-1-52475-902-5
eBook ISBN: 978-1-52475-903-2

Printed in China

Design by Angelina Cheney

10 9 8 7 6 5 4 3 2 1

First Edition